E-preneur

From Wall Street to Wiki:
Make money from the
changing online world

Richard J. Goossen, PhD

This edition first published in Great Britain 2009 by

Crimson Publishing, a division of Crimson Business Ltd
Westminster House
Kew Road
Richmond
Surrey
TW9 2ND

First published in the United States by Career Press,
Inc in 2008

First Published in Great Britain by Crimson Publishing
in 2009

A catalogue record for this book is available from the
British library.

ISBN 978 1 85458 458 8

Printed and bound by Mega Printing, Turkey

Dedicated to

Brenda, Brooke, Matthias, Neil, and Kaylyn.

Acknowledgements

First and foremost, I would like to thank the various individuals whose interviews contributed to the research for this book: Chris Breikss, co-founder and director, S6 Marketing; Fred David, a leading strategic management thinker and author; Larry Farrell of Farrell International; John Fluevog and Stephen Bailey of Fluevog Shoes; Jeff Howe of *Wired Magazine*; Rita McGrath of the School of Business, Columbia University; Mike Sikorsky, founder and CEO, Cambrian House; Jeff Timmons, professor of Entrepreneurship at Babson College; and Michael Tippett, co-founder and CEO of NowPublic. Although these exceptionally talented individuals are extremely busy, they were generous with their time and insights. In several instances, follow-up interviews were required and generously granted. I appreciated their willingness to contribute to this undertaking.

I am grateful for the assistance provided through the Center for Entrepreneurial Leaders, School of Business, Trinity Western University. My research assistants at the center provided invaluable help with research, and transcribing interviews: Michelle Sui, and Doug van Spronsen.

I would like to thank Michael Pye, Michael Fitzgibbon, Kirsten Dalley, and Kate Henches at Career Press for turning the original manuscript into a book; their expert insights and professional guidance were extremely helpful. In addition, my literary agent, Bill Gladstone, Waterside Productions, Cardiff-by-the-Sea, Calif., provided highly professional advice and insight on how to transform the idea for this book to a completed product.

Richard J. Goossen
Founder and CEO
Crowdpreneur Networks, Inc.
www.crowdpreneur.com
&
Founder and Director
Centre for Entrepreneurial Leaders
School of Business
Trinity Western University
www.EntrepreneurialLeaders.com

Contents

Introduction

What Is the "New Virtual Marketplace" and Why Does It Matter?

Many established businesspeople believe they have already integrated the Internet into their businesses. To them, the Internet is a portal for long lists of impersonal e-mails, or an information highway complete with Web pages that look like desktop billboards. It is a more convenient tool for doing things they have always done.

But these businesspeople may not fully realize that the Internet is changing, and that its new developments have a huge impact on every business. With its continually evolving technology, the Internet has the potential to further transform businesses through an interactive model that promotes entrepreneurial activity and transforms relationships with customers. The new virtual marketplace provides an international group of people willing to collaborate, offer loyalty, engage in dialogue, envision possibilities, and co-create with companies. It is the most dynamic and widespread community this world has ever seen. And that is why the new virtual marketplace matters.

From Web 1.0 to Web 2.0 and the Wiki

The Internet caused significant societal changes in the mid-1990s when it presented itself as an "information highway"—a means of displaying information widely and effortlessly and conducting various levels of e-commerce. Today that iteration of the Internet is widely known as "Web 1.0." It was an initial equalizer whereby small companies could market their wares globally, often from the company founder's basement. Companies and their investors scrambled to stake out territory in this new marketplace, where the control of the medium was more important than product expertise. Jeff Bezos, the founder of *www.amazon.com*, for example, is an expert on the Internet rather than an originally devoted bookseller. He understands the role of technology and is able to apply his sales expertise to the distribution of different products and services—including books, DVDs and more—to an expanding customer base.

A wide range of new companies and paradigms, such as *www.eBay.com*, flourished during Web 1.0. Yet, at the same time, many other companies floundered and disappeared from the landscape. Not every idea with an Internet angle was viable. Moreover, Internet businesses were hit hard by the dot-com bust of March 2000; the events of 9-11 in 2001 added a further chill. These factors doused investor exuberance and forced the Internet to undergo a significant structural renaissance. Amid this renaissance, a few of the original companies emerged on top by addressing practical needs and opportunities with innovative methods and technological expertise. These companies, most notably *www.google.com*, were able to establish viable and highly profitable business models on the Internet—business models that outlasted the disastrous years.

In retrospect, Web 1.0 spawned some initial forms of mass collaboration. One notable example of collaboration was the creation of Linux software through "open sourcing." (Linux was created as a free software system to be continuously improved online through mass collaboration for everyone's mutual benefit.) Another impetus to online collaboration is the "wiki," which is a Website that allows users to edit and create pages to the host computer from a Web browser without any additional software ("wiki" is a Hawaiian word that means "fast"). Of course, the term is most widely popularized as a prefix in one of the world's most-trafficked sites (*www.wikipedia.com*). However, the notion of mass collaboration truly took shape in the next phase of the Internet—what many are now calling Web 2.0. If

Web 1.0 was about information, Web 2.0 is about collaboration and community.

The pervasive nature of collaboration in the current online environment is reflected by the fact that six of the top 15 traffic-generating sites on the Internet are "User Generated Interface" sites. A prime example is Wikipedia, the online encyclopedia that has over 2.2 million articles contributed by volunteers (and anyone can join). Another form of collaboration is online communities such as *www.facebook.com*, the college-oriented social networking site with almost 100 million members.

As these examples demonstrate, we live in an age of accelerating technological and social change. *Time* magazine clearly identified the source of these online communities and the modern need for self-expression when it proclaimed "You" as Person of the Year for 2006.[1] The newsweekly noted, "We're looking at an explosion of productivity and innovation, and it's just getting started, as millions of minds that would otherwise have drowned in obscurity get backhauled into the global intellectual community."[2]

These exciting developments in the world of Web 2.0 have burst into mainstream business with reports of the sale of Internet businesses. The site *www.youtube.com* was recently sold for $1.5 billion to Google after having been in existence for only a few years. The founders reaped an astounding windfall. In addition, Rupert Murdoch's News Corp. bought *www.myspace.com* from its founders for $580 million.

Why are these expressions of online community making astronomical windfalls? In his recent bestseller *The Tipping Point: How Little Things Can Make a Big Difference*, Malcolm Gladwell notes, "In a world dominated by isolation and immunity, understanding [the] principles of word of mouth is more important than ever."[3]

On a more drastic scale, Tapscott and Williams write in *Wikinomics: How Mass Collaboration Changes Everything*, "But the new participation will also cause great upheaval, dislocation, and danger for societies, corporations, and individuals that fail to keep up with relentless change."[4] Thus, a dynamic human search for connection, equality, and collaboration within relationships is now rapidly driving a demanding market. That's where this Internet idea takes flight.

The relational developments promoted by Web 2.0 affect how all businesses, whether Internet-based or not, perceive and interact with customers. Traditionally, businesses perceived their customer base as an audience. Businesses talked to customers through television or newspaper ads, billboards, pamphlets, product packaging, and other one-way-street methods. Customers responded by deciding whether or not to purchase the product. Occasionally customers talked back by returning a faulty product, calling an information line, participating in a telephone survey, or writing a letter of commendation or complaint. Yet, like audience members in a theatrical production, customers' responses were limited to clapping, booing, and the odd "letter to the director" following an exceptional or horrible experience.

Then Web 2.0 started changing people's expectations of the customer-supplier relationship. Suddenly the audience stepped up on stage and started taking over, telling the actors where to go and what to say. Now audience members are becoming the directors and script-writers and set-designers, and they are making up plays of their own. The entire audience, on the stage, has started exercising control—and businesses have to obey at the risk of losing revenue. This, in simplified terms, is the root concept of "crowd power."

In this upside-down environment, some businesses have capitalized on the direction of the crowd. Instead of cowering in a corner or trying to yell out the old lines, these businesses have embraced the new market by using customers' advice and ideas to build or improve their products and services. These businesses demonstrate what I call "crowdpreneurship."

The word "crowdpreneur" is a contraction of "crowd-empowered entrepreneur." It refers to an individual or organization that uses the strategy of online crowd empowerment in its various forms (collective intelligence, mass collaboration, crowdsourcing, and others) in the pursuit of an entrepreneurial venture. In other words, "crowdpreneur" is shorthand for applying entrepreneurial principles to this new area of innovation in the Web 2.0 world.

The intention of this book is to focus in detail on the companies that are actively succeeding as crowdpreneurs in the new virtual marketplace, rather than to offer cursory reviews that simply compile surface-level information. In order to understand these companies fully, I interviewed the founders in depth. In particular, I interviewed the founders of Fluevog Shoes, NowPublic, and Cambrian House. In addition, I interviewed a number of key thought leaders and I have separately highlighted a key interview with Jeff Howe, who coined the term "crowdsourcing."

Mad Crowds and Smart Mobs

What is the significance of an online community—or crowd—in relation to collective action? After all, we typically hear of "mobs" and mass hysteria, innumerable atrocities and misjudgments happening as a result of large groups uniting with a cause, whether in John Wayne Westerns with scenes of vigilantes at the sheriff's door or in the brutal slayings motivated by tribal and ethnic rivalries in African nations. What is different in an online environment? We must examine more closely the distinctions between unwise and wise crowds.

One common starting point for a discussion of the action of crowds is Charles Mackay's book *Extraordinary Popular Delusions and the Madness of Crowds*, published in 1841.[5] Mackay provides an entertaining history of crowd stupidity, and notes, "Popular delusions began so early, spread so widely, and have lasted so long, that instead of two to three volumes, fifty would scarcely suffice to detail their history."[6] He reviews well-known manias throughout the ages, such as "The Mississippi Scheme, The South-Sea Bubble, The Tulipomania [sic] and The Alchymists [sic]." The tales recounted by Mackay share an eerie similarity with investment-related manias that have arisen since the time he published his book, demonstrating that crowd-inspired foolishness has not diminished with time.

One of the investment manias he describes is the Mississippi Scheme. The scheme was orchestrated in 1719 and 1720 by an Englishman, John Law, who was based in France at that time. The French Parliament granted to the Mississippi Company "the exclusive privilege of trading to the East Indies, China, and the South Seas, and to all the possessions of the French East India Company."[7] John Law had peddled a series of investment offerings, and in 1719 he made 50,000 shares avaliable. Mackay explains, "The prospects now held out by Law were most magnificent. He promised a yearly dividend of two hundred lives upon each share of five hundred, which, as the shares were paid for in billets d' etat, at their nominal value, but worth only 100 livres, was at the rate of about 120 percent profit."[8] Enthusiastic investors flocked to him. Needless to say, the grandiose returns promised by Law did not materialize.

Another tantalizing tale is tied up in the history of tulips in the Netherlands. Mackay explains that by the 1630s tulips became so popular that "it was deemed a proof of bad taste in any man of fortune to be without a collection of them."[9] (Apparently, the tulip was a forerunner of luxury foreign import vehicles.) As the rage continued, "the middle classes of society, and merchants and shopkeepers, even of modest means, began to vie with each other in the rarity of these flowers and the preposterous prices they paid for them."[10] As is typical in such a mania, there is no foresight that the rise might be followed by a drop, and each person is emboldened by tales of others who have made a fortune while others dithered. "In 1634, the rage among the Dutch to possess them was so great that the ordinary industry of the country was neglected, and the population, even to its lowest dregs, embarked in the tulip trade."[11] This reminds me of the cliché that when taxi drivers and dentists are making money in the real estate or stock market, the market is about to drop.

What, then, should be decided about crowds of people and their actions? Mackay laments, "Men, it has been well said, think in herds; it will be seen that they go mad in herds, while they only recover their senses slowly, and one by one."[12] Although Mackay defined these groups of people as "crowds," is this a fair representation of the dynamics of all group interaction? Not necessarily. There is a clear difference between investment manias and independent-minded, though collective, action.

Howard Rheingold, a leading writer on the social implications of technology, authored a book in 2002 under the title *Smart Mobs: The Next Social Revolution.* He intentionally uses the term "mobs," which generally has a negative connotation in relation to group activity. Yet Rheingold describes the mob as smart. He explains that smart mobs "consist of people who are able to act in concert even if they don't know each other."[13] At the time of writing his book in 2002, Rheingold was also optimistic about the positive power of the online crowd's opinions. For example, one component of Web 1.0 was the development of so-called reputation systems. Buyers and sellers could be rated on eBay and Amazon and so on. Thus strangers could conduct business online with a high degree of transaction comfort despite the fact that they had never met in person. This was not a new human desire, but simply an easier way to get results. Rheingold points out, "Today's [circa 2002] online reputation systems are computer-based technologies that make it possible to manipulate in new and powerful ways an old and essential human trait."[14] Rheingold identified groups of people online as having value; however, at the time of his writing the true value of collaborative behavior in an online environment was not yet fully analyzed.

A turning point in understanding the value of crowds—both online and offline—was the 2004 publication of James Surowiecki's *The Wisdom of the Crowds*. His provocative conclusion was that "under the right circumstances, groups are remarkably intelligent, and are often smarter than the smartest people in them."[15] At first glance this proposition appears counterintuitive; we are familiar with the mob, the crowd, and the irrational outcomes that appear to occur. However, Surowiecki provides a logical analysis as to how crowds of individuals—in particular circumstances—are superior to any one individual. Surowiecki states his objective: "The argument of this book is that chasing the expert is a mistake, and a costly one at that."[16]

Surowiecki focuses on three types of problems in which the wisdom of crowds is helpful. There are "cognition problems," which are problems with definitive solutions (that is, Who will win the Super Bowl?). There are "coordination problems," which require members of a group to coordinate their behavior in order to reach a resolution (that is, What is the best route to a destination in heavy traffic?). Finally, there are "cooperation problems," in which the challenge is to motivate "self-interested, distrustful people to work together, even when narrow self-interest would dictate that no individual should take part."[17] (That is, How can we deal with the problem of pollution?)

Surowiecki makes a critical distinction in his conclusion regarding the wisdom of crowds. He states that the "wisdom of the crowds" is best in situations in which the individuals are acting apart from one another, but are all addressing the same issue. Then the individual responses can be averaged out with the outcome typically superior to that of any single individual. Surowiecki writes, "With most things, the average is mediocrity. With decision making, it's often excellence. You could say it's as if we've been programmed to be collectively smart."[18]

The Internet crowd is a prime example of Surowiecki's ideal situation because it combines interaction with individuality: though a chat room or blog may contain a mass amount of comments, or a Web page may have millions of users at once, each of those users is likely sitting alone with his or her computer screen rather than sitting in an auditorium full of like-minded people. In other words, the Internet "crowds" are masses of individuals with a variety of opinions on any given stance. Their meeting place is technological, not physical. They are able to communicate en masse without being physically present in the same place. Thus, as Surowiecki emphasizes, they are able to retain their individual judgments while working together.

The Evolution of Crowd Power

The acceptance and understanding of the wisdom of the crowd has now begun to evolve into practical applications of the crowd power concept. The notion of crowd power took root due to two underlying factors in society. First, the rise of user-generated media such as blogs and traffic-generating Websites (that is, Wikipedia, MySpace, and YouTube) demonstrated the power of gathering ideas from the Internet crowd. Secondly, the traditional distinction between producers and consumers ha become increasingly blurry. The Web 2.0 world was and is the world's equalizer—and the result is that today's technology makes it possible to enlist ever-larger numbers of non-technical people to become involved in online contributions. The notion of a crowd (or group of people) being able to work together to achieve a particular purpose in an online environment has spawned a plethora of competing, overlapping terminology.

Open Innovation

One approach to categorizing online group activity is to focus on "open innovation."[19] This is a term promoted by Henry Chesbrough, a professor and the executive director at the Center for Open Innovation at Berkeley.[20] The central idea behind open innovation is that in a world of widely distributed knowledge, companies cannot afford to rely entirely on their own research, but should instead buy or license processes or inventions (that is, patents) from other companies. In addition, internal inventions not being used in a firm's business should be taken outside the company (for example, through licensing, joint ventures, or spin-offs). In contrast, "closed innovation" refers to processes that limit the use of internal knowledge within a company and make little or no use of external knowledge. A company that demonstrates open innovation is InnoCentive, which will be discussed later in the book.

One widespread example of open innovation is open-source software. An "open source" program is one in which the source code is available for all to see.[21] Anyone can use and alter the software code to his or her requirements (under a general public license) without a fee. This fosters a collaborative approach to software development such that users improve and extend the core by adding their own work back into the project for free. There is usually an enthusiastic free support network, and the development of the program is often faster and more user-oriented than the development of competing programs for sale. A popular example of this is the Firefox Web browser.

Mass Collaboration

Another well-known term is "mass collaboration." This form of collective action occurs when large numbers of people work independently on a single project, often modular in its nature. A key aspect distinguishing mass collaboration from other forms of large-scale collaboration is that the collaborative process is mediated by the content being created—as opposed to being mediated by direct social interaction.[22] This term was recently popularized in the subtitle to Tapscott and Williams's book, *Wikinomics: How Mass Collaboration Changes Everything.*

Collective Intelligence

One term that has been around for a long time is "collective intelligence." Thomas W. Malone, professor at the MIT Sloan

School of Management, states that the goal of the MIT Center for Collective Intelligence is to address the question, "How can people and computers be connected so that collectively they act more intelligently than any person, group, or computer has ever done before?"[23] The term collective intelligence was initially popularized by Tim O'Reilly, the Internet thought leader who helped develop the term "Web 2.0." The impetus for this "collective intelligence" movement was the development of open source software. O'Reilly states, "Open source software leverages the power of network effects, enlightened self-interest, and the architecture of participation."[24] He ties collective intelligence into the "network effect"—how networks grow as a result of the value of the connections they make. According to O'Reilly, "To the extent that any Web 2.0 company uses network effects to its fullest potential, {the company has} harnessed collective intelligence."[25] O'Reilly originally attempted to define Web 2.0 and collective intelligence in a September 2005 article. He wrote, "It is hard to create boundaries around terms; instead, they are pointers to general meanings of the concept [of Web 2.0]."[26]

The Threads of Crowd Power

There are a number of crowd-related terms that have at their base an element of the power of the crowd. As well, the strategy of harnessing crowd wisdom goes under different names, ranging from "crowd clout" to "crowdsourcing." "Crowd power" is perhaps the most generic term. The term "crowd clout," for example, focuses on consumer activism in its definition: an "online grouping of citizens/consumers for a specific cause, be it political, civic or commercial, aimed at everything from bringing down politicians to forcing suppliers to fork over discounts."[27]

Meanwhile, the term "crowdsourcing" is gaining popular momentum. Jeff Howe wrote an article called "The Rise of Crowdsourcing" in the June 2006 issue of *Wired Magazine,* and it has been a buzzword ever since.[28] Howe defines it as a process wherein a "company or institution takes a job traditionally performed by a designated agent (usually an employee) and outsources it to an undefined, generally large group of people over the Internet." He also provides a "soundbyte" version: "The application of Open Source principles to fields outside of software." The basic business idea behind crowdsourcing is to tap into the collective intelligence of the public at large in order to complete business-related tasks that a company would normally either perform itself or outsource to a third-party provider.[29] The various benefits include free labor as well as expanding the range of idea contribution and expertise. The process also secures customer or client contribution to the development of products, and thus enhances customer loyalty.

Blogger Josh Catone breaks down the concept of sourcing the crowd into three categories.[30] First, he believes crowdsourcing can apply to the creation of content for a site, which is then referred to as a "user-generated interface" (that is, *www.wikipedia.com* and *www.cambrianhouse.com*). A second form of crowdsourcing relates to organization—using the crowd's choices to help organize and prioritize data. PageRank (used by Google) for example, does this through a link analysis algorithm. Another example of using crowdsourcing to organize information is found at *www.stumbleupon.com*, which helps people "discover new sites." A third form of crowdsourcing has to do with prediction. By polling the crowd, you can determine what is popular and what is not—for example, visit *www.digg.com*, which lists news stories based on readers indicating whether they "digg"—approve of them or not. Regardless of how the term is defined, the potential for crowdsourcing to be used in a powerful way in developing rapidly. What is the future of crowdsourcing? As Jeff Howe told me, "Today is 'Day 1' with respect to crowdsourcing. The concept is in its infancy, though it is clearly starting to send shock waves."[31]

The different variations on the theme of crowd wisdom and power will (for the purposes of this book) be treated as threads that are part of the general concept of "crowd power." I prefer to use this term. The term has been deployed by NowPublic .com, a firm that is at the forefront of so-called citizenship journalism. NowPublic's tag line is "crowd-powered media." They describe their approach as follows: "By harnessing the wisdom of crowds and tapping into the news-creating potential of the hundreds of millions of Internet users, bloggers and photography enthusiasts, NowPublic is changing the way news is made and distributed."[32] I will refer to companies that tap into the various threads as "crowd-powered" companies, regardless of the particular form of crowd power they have adopted. More important to my analysis is the extent to which crowd-powered behavior is used in relation to the business model of a firm. This will determine whether or not a firm is crowdpreneurial.

The Generational Divide

Who most readily recognizes the opportunities of crowd power in the new virtual marketplace? Not surprisingly, a person's age—and thus generational cohort—will greatly impact his or her view of technology. Clearly the opportunities of the Web 2.0 world are more familiar to those in the younger demographic, because, as has been true throughout history, the young are embracing new technologies, and by extension are among the first to exploit them. For example, while a "social community" online is an oddity to Baby Boomers and Traditionalists, it is a lifeline for Gen Xers and Yers.

An understanding of Web 2.0 across generational lines is vital in order to fully seize entrepreneurial opportunities. Specifically, the launch of a Web 2.0 venture may require the intuition of Gen Yers, the skills of Gen Xers, the managerial expertise of Baby Boomers, and the financing of the Traditionalists. Thus all generations must understand both themselves and others. Along those lines, each generation needs to grasp its unique strengths and shortcomings in order to better function in the Web 2.0 world.

Opportunities, depend greatly on an individual's generational vantage point. Although acceptance of change and the pursuit of innovation are not neatly divided along generational lines, the two factors do provide a shorthand approach for basic analysis. David Foot, a well-respected demographer, notes, "Age is the best forecasting tool because it is guaranteed to change."[33] He believes each individual is a member of a "cohort," but "most of us think of ourselves as individuals and underestimate how much we have in common with fellow members of our cohort."[34]

Putting that into a Web 2.0 context, I have analyzed four generations, each of which responds differently to the Internet. First, there are "Traditionalists," born between 1922 and 1945 (62 to 85 years old). Internet use and familiarity in their generation is sporadic, and generally superficial. Traditionalists most likely use the Internet to e-mail grandkids and do online reading. Second, there are "Baby Boomers," born between 1946 and 1964 (41 to 61 years old). In the prime of their careers, many people from this generation are Web 1.0-focused users. The other important thing to know about them is that there are so many of them (the single largest group was in 1961). Canada, the United States, Australia and New Zealand had booms—partly because the countries were immigrant receivers in those years, and immigrants tended to be in their 20s, the prime childbearing age. The U.S. boom was from 1946 to 1964, during a time when people could afford large families: World War II had just ended, the economy was robust, and the future was full of promise. The boom ended because, among a variety of reasons, more women entered the workforce and the birth control pill became available. The Baby Boomer generation likely has some inconsistent familiarity with Web 2.0, depending upon individuals' job requirements and personal preferences.

Most "Gen Xers," however, born from 1965 to 1980 (27 to 41 years old), embrace technology and the Internet as a way to maintain control of their lives; they grew up in the midst of Web 1.0. Lastly, there are the "Gen Yers," born after 1980 (26 and younger), who are immersed in Internet technology. Many of them have grown up alongside Web 2.0, subconsciously accepting its mentality as a reality of everyday life. They build and maintain an overwhelming number of relationships online.

Obviously, a gap of misunderstanding exists between the former and latter generations.So, why does this matter? Actually, an understanding of Web 2.0 that spans generational lines is vital to fully seizing entrepreneurial opportunities. In other words, the launch of a Web 2.0 venture may require the intuitiveness of Gen Yers, the skills of Gen Xers, the managerial expertise of Baby Boomers, and the financing of the Traditionalists. Thus, in order for such a venture to be successful, generations must understand both themselves and others. Moreover, each generation needs to grasp its unique strengths and shortcomings in order to better function in the Web 2.0 world. For example, not all Gen Yers are truly part of the "Net Gen"—some have embraced online technology more thoroughly than their peers. These late adapters need to be brought into the Web 2.0 fold. Gen Yers should also recognize their unique perspectives and seek to build bridges with other generations.

The drive behind Web 2.0 comes primarily from Gen Yers, and secondarily from Gen Xers. As a 47-year-old Baby Boomer adjunct professor, I teach Gen Yers (primarily 22- to 24-year-olds). My students generally don't read the major daily newspapers or watch the six o'clock news, and they think "60 Minutes" is a time limit on someone's use of the Internet. The Gen Yers get information from visiting their favorite Websites, following a series of blogs, joining various online communities, and emailing or "facebooking" interesting tidbits and videos to their friends.

From the outside, Baby Boomers and Traditionalists can't understand Gen Yers' cultural differences. Baby Boomers ask, "Who has time to create and read blogs, join communities, contribute ideas, post silly videos for strangers, and the like?" Meanwhile, Gen Yers muse that people from the older generation have time to bury their faces in the daily paper or come home and watch TV programs. The key point is to anticipate demographic change and long-term trends; in fact, the further you look into the future, the more important these trends are.

E-preneur—From Wall Street to Wiki

In today's world, successful entrepreneurs are "e-Preneurs," those who are able to recognize and tap into the depth of opportunity the emerging Internet marketplace provides. E-preneurs stop seeing customers as audience members and start seeing them as collaborators—creative directors, commentators, critics, inventors. E-preneurs apply the realities of Web 2.0 and crowd power to their business models, using these emerging opportunities to redefine the way their companies operate. E-preneurs combine an understanding of e-commerce with entrepreneurial principles.

Today's Web 2.0 environment is ripe with opportunities. In later 2007 one report noted, "It seems to be boomtime again in the dot-com industry after the lean years that followed the first dot-com crash in [early] 2001."[35] The purpose of this book is to allow you to navigate between the metaphorical worlds of Wall Street and the wiki. How do you do this? The starting point is to follow the five steps of the crowdpreneur in order to succeed in the new virtual marketplace.

Navigating the Book

In this book, I have no desire to discuss ground already covered. I am also not attempting to define the "why" of crowd power or spend too much time setting boundaries. Instead, I focus on the practical aspects of the threads of crowd power. I have worked with new ventures for more than 20 years, and thus my primary interest is how principles actually work in the marketplace.

The format of the book mirrors the process required to successfully launch a new venture. Its five chapters are the steps required to succeed as a crowdpreneur in the new virtual marketplace: adopting the entrepreneurial lens; pursuing opportunities through innovation; conducting a careful feasibility analysis of the opportunity; developing an effective crowd-powered business model; and executing a careful plan for financing and growing the company.

The profiles and interviews following each chapter relate to themes evident throughout the entire book and not only the content of the particular chapter. I do quote from these profiles and interviews selectively throughout the book in order to supplement my analysis of key issues. However, I have intentionally presented the interviews with leading thinkers or company founders in their entirety in order to offer a stand-alone perspective or opinion on issues for your reference.

Finally, in keeping with the spirit of the e-Preneur or crowdpreneur concept, this is not just a book; it's the portal to an online community at *www.crowdpreneur.com*. Moreover, our Website is not just a series of pages of static information about the book; rather, it's an opportunity for you—the user—to collaborate with myself and other users. In the process of writing this book, I have collected a variety of online opinions instead of simply touting my own. Now that the book is published, you can contribute by writing your own insights about each section of the book online, thus creating an expanding, dynamic version of the story for which this book is merely a springboard. Join us at *www.crowdpreneur.com* to see the crowdpreneur concept in action.

Top 10 Buzzwords From the Web 2.0 Summit

Short Form and Long Meaning

Every gathering has its own unique lingo that acts a barrier to full understanding for the uninitiated—somewhat like a lawyer's jargon. Here's my list of the top buzzwords from the 2007 summit.

1. The Long Tail: This phrase was popularized by Chris Anderson in his book *The Long Tail: Why the Future of Business is Selling Less of More* (2006). The basic idea is that the Internet allows companies to sell profitability to the long part of the distribution curve ("the long tail"), which is a large number of very small niche markets (exemplified by the success of businesses such as Amazon).

2. The Wisdom of the Crowd: This phrase is based on James Surowiecki's book *The Wisdom of Crowds* (2004). Surowiecki explains compellingly how a crowd is often able to come up with better solutions to problems than any single individual. This concept corroborates the concept of "harnessing collective intelligence," one of Tim O'Reilly's core components of Web 2.0. More generally, the notion of the "wisdom of the crowd" ties in with related phrases such as "mass collaboration" and "crowdsourcing."

3. Network Effects: A network's value rises based on the extent to which it becomes increasingly interconnected. Once a certain critical mass of users has been achieved, then others will join in because of the value of the existing interconnected community (consider the Facebook community, for example). Simply stated, network effects are the way in which networks grow as a result of the value of the connections they make.

4. Mashup: This is one word that people just like to say because it rolls off the tongue nicely. A mashup is a Web application that combines data from more than one source into a single integrated tool. One example is the use of cartographic data from Google Maps to add location information to restaurant data from a city information site. The result is a new and distinct Web service that neither of the original sources contemplated.

5. CPM: This acronym was thrown about regularly at the summit, CPM is an abbreviation for "cost per mille (that is, per thousand)," and is commonly used as a benchmark measurement in advertising. Different forms of advertising, from television to online, can be purchased on the basis of what it costs to show the ad to a thousand viewers.

6. Scalability: A key issue for a new venture is whether or not its Website can be ramped up quickly in order to handle extreme use and rampant popularity. Of course, from an entrepreneurial standpoint, you don't want to be too optimistic—this could be an expensive fantasy. On the other hand, the height of irony would be that the sheer and instant popularity of a site overwhelms the servers, the site crashes, and people lose confidence in the company. One of the MySpace founders recalls driving around Silicon Valley one weekend, in the early days of MySpace, desperately trying to buy servers. He and other founders then had to load the servers into a truck and haul them back to their office as additional support for the popular site.

7. Viral: This word is a virtual mantra, in that for companies to succeed they need to have viral uptake. In other words, the use of a site spreads like a virus, passed on from one person to another. As a result, advertising is viewed as both terribly expensive, and somehow conceding defeat that the preferred mode of viral marketing is not working. A successful site does not rely on paid promotion, but rather on making the site offering attractive enough that it gets passed on among contacts voluntarily.

8. Price per Unique: A unique visitor is a statistic describing a unit of traffic to a Website, counting each visitor only once in the time frame of the report. The objective is to separate the number of individuals visiting a site from the simple gross count of the number of hits on a site. This is a vital distinction for advertisers, as it reveals true audience size. The unique visitors are tracked either by requiring all visitors to log in to the site or by placing a cookie on each visitor's computer.

9. In the Cloud: This phrase relates to another key Web 2.0 element, which is "the Internet as platform." The basic idea is that your data is no longer on your desktop, but rather in cyberspace, accessible from any computer. For example, Google's applications rely on the storage of data on servers in the "cloud." A related use of the term is to talk about "cloud computing," with the idea of relying on Web-based applications and storing data in the cloud of the Internet. Of course, a company such as Google is providing Web-based applications (that is, shared documents).

10. Monetize: Possibly to counteract the view that the current interest in Web 2.0 is devoid of a viable commercial context, many presenters at the Summit talked about "monetization." In other words, people were trying to explain how to make money from Web 2.0 businesses. Specifically, monetization is about how to make money from the traffic to a site: This is largely related to selling ads or generating subscription fees.

Top 10 Quotes From the Web 2.0 Summit

With so many speakers at the summit, several pithy comments inspired the audience. Here's my list of favorite quotes:

1. **J. Craig Venter,** a leading genomic research scientist (J. Craig Venter Institute) and author of *A Life Decoded: My Genome—My Life*: "The future is here; it is just not evenly distributed yet."

2. **Evan Williams,** cofounder of Twitter, used a quote he attributed to Tantek Celik: "The cognitive load of an individual is related to the number of clicks." In other words, make your Website very simple.

3. **Mike Moritz,** Sequoia Capital, highlighted a classic entrepreneurial maxim of customer focus: "The goal of all great companies is to enable people to do something for themselves." This is a simple restatement of where a company's focus should be: on the end user.

4. **Chris DeWolfe,** cofounder of MySpace, now with News Corp., stressed the following: "A company needs to do only one thing very, very well in order to maintain its competitive position."

5. **Meg Whitman,** CEO of eBay, sanguinely noted (in view of past eBay acquisitions) that "the price of inaction is far greater than making a costly mistake."

6. **Morgan Webb,** the host of X-Play on G4, talked about the important aspect of the "immersive experience" and "social experience" for Gen Y on the Web and described how games fill "the black hole of social life." She made this comment in a matter-of-fact way. Although it's likely not disputable, many see it as a sad commentary on the state of social life.

7. **Jane McGonigal,** a game designer/researcher at the Institute for the Future, explained the significance of online games as "a means of finding purpose, being happy, and building community." In other words, people continue to search for some meaning in their lives—now they simply have another means of finding it.

8. **Joel Hyatt** of Current TV focuses on allowing people to effectively watch TV via the Internet. He summarized his approach as follows: "We don't want to bring the dumbness of TV to the Internet; we want to bring the magic of the Internet to TV."

9. **John Doerr,** Kleiner Perkins, and a director of Google noted that one of the company's keys to success is "its maniacal focus on the user experience." The success of the Web 2.0 juggernaut is not simply its leading technology, but also the company's ability to execute its program.

10. **Doerr spoke** passionately about one particular social cause—global warming—which he called a "planetary emergency." What can be done? Doerr provided a great clarion call: "Never underestimate the power of a handful of entrepreneurs to change the world."

PROFILE

Tim O'Reilly, Web 2.0 Guru

Tim O'Reilly is the founder and principal of O'Reilly Media. His firm coined the term "Web 2.0" and has hosted the pivotal Web 2.0 summits and Web 2.0 conferences in Silicon Valley. O'Reilly is among the most influential thought leaders in the Web 2.0 field. He has been referred to as one of the gurus of the participation age. This profile is based on my recent interview with Him.[1]

What Is "Collective Intelligence"?

O'Reilly has identified a number of important concepts that are connected to the idea of harnessing collective intelligence and what is meant by Web 2.0.

First is the idea of what he has called the open source paradigm shift. In today's environment, there is a process of commoditization whereby the value is going out of many classes of software that people used to pay for. But there is still value; it is a question of where on the stack the value is located. This led O'Reilly to rethink the nature of the Web and to come up with some new ideas around what is now referred to as Web 2.0. Moving up the stack includes using the Internet as a platform and software as a service, and harnessing collective intelligence. By contrast, there is what O'Reilly calls moving down the stack, such as the "Data is the Next Intel Inside" concept. This analysis is based on what Clayton Christensen calls "The Law of Conservation of Attractive Profits" (see the discussion of Christensen's writings in Step #2 under "Classic Insights on Innovation"). The basic point is that every time you see something for free, then something else is becoming expensive. The impetus for this development was Linux and other types of open source software, which was a disruptive force that changed the game. Open source software leverages the power of network effects, enlightened self-interest, and the architecture of participation. But the trend didn't stop there. O'Reilly noticed that many of the most successful Websites were also harnessing user participation and the network effects that ensue.[2]

Second, the Internet is the platform. O'Reilly explains that once you realize that we're in a new platform era, you have to ask yourself what makes for success on that platform. On the PC, it was all about building applications for individual user productivity. On the network, it's about building applications that enable shared activity. But that's not just explicit collaboration. It also includes implicit collaboration.

O'Reilly's view is that to the extent that any Web 2.0 company uses network effects to their fullest potential, they have harnessed collective intelligence. Google's realization that links were a kind of user-generated "voting" on the best site for a topic (such as PageRank) and could be used to deliver better search results, was arguably the real beginning of the Web 2.0 revolution. But each in their own way, Yahoo, eBay, Amazon, Craigslist, and Wikipedia all are showing different ways to harness collective intelligence to add value. Amazon, for example, has doggedly and persistently pursued the notion of users adding value. They didn't have a built-in architecture of participation, but they worked on it. O'Reilly explains that "the key is to work together; harnessing creative intelligence is the heart of Web 2.0." He also notes that the key question for companies to get involved in Web 2.0 is to ask, "What can we do on a shared network?"[3] The objective is to build networks that get better as more people use them; this is the basis for the next generation of Internet companies.

What Is Web 2.0?

Web 2.0 has become a bandied-about buzzword. In his article titled "What is Web 2.0" of September 2005,[4] O'Reilly attempted to clarify what he meant by Web 2.0, including the nature of harnessing collective intelligence. O'Reilly acknowledged in my interview with him that, "It is hard to create boundaries around terms; instead, they are pointers to a general meaning of the concept."

Of relevance to this book is to separate "collective intelligence," which is used by O'Reilly, from "crowdsourcing," which is the term deployed by Jeff Howe. O'Reilly believes that they are overlapping terms, and that the boundaries are quite vague. He indicated that one key differentiator is the degree of intentionality from the group of people whose input is being sought. O'Reilly explains: "My understanding of crowdsourcing is that it is the process of building on aggregate work, such as in the case of Wikipedia, where a group of people 'swarm' to build each entry, building on the work of preceding visitors."[5]

By contrast, his view of collective intelligence is that the collaboration need not be explicit. In other words, a company is organizing input for a particular purpose, but each individual may not even know the or she is contributing. For example, people don't think of themselves as contributing to Google when they make a Web link, but they are doing so nonetheless. O'Reilly argues that "Collective intelligence often involves algorithms to extract the value of the shared work."[6]

Does Web 2.0 shape or change the way we think? According to O'Reilly, "I think the Web does change people, but then many forms of technology, (such as TV) change people. There are, however, some qualitative differences in the way the Internet has changed people's lives. You can now get information at the drop of a hat."[7]

Succeeding at Harnessing Collective Intelligence

Regardless of the particular definition, the critical question is to determine how a company can be successful at harnessing collective intelligence. O'Reilly suggests that there are six factors that contribute to an organization's success.

First, a company must get to critical mass with respect to data accumulation as soon as possible in order to effectively prevent others from entering the market. This is why eBay is hard to dislodge from their preeminent position, rather than because they have the best technology. For example, why can they not get into China? Some one else was there first.

Second, a company that gets into a market first must then take advantage of the network effect and start building up its database. A company must realize that value lies in data accumulation and not the software. As Dan Bricklin explains, there are three ways to build a large database: pay people to do it, get volunteers to perform the task, or obtain data as a byproduct of selfish intent of the individual.[8] It is this last category that is critical. This is the "walk-in" by users who contribute to a database simply as a result of the way it has been designed.

Third, a company needs to figure out how to make their Website viral. In order to do this, a company needs to focus on the network effect. For example, Facebook opened up access to a lot of their core services, and this allows people to build complementary applications. But one thing they control as a choke point is communication with users.

Fourth, it is important for a company to find simple ways to get users to participate without a conscious decision. Flickr has demonstrated this by making "public" the default and "private" as the option. Determining the choice of defaults as to how people participate in a site is quite significant. Another example is Skype; they don't ask you if you want to share your bandwidth. It's just part of the design of the product. A key is to get people to share data without meaning to give it.

A fifth point is for a company to think beyond the obvious uses of data. Breakthroughs will come from seeing meaning in data that people didn't realize was there. Companies need to appreciate that where people spend their money is a vote. In other words, meaning is already encoded, but it just has to be mined. There is a lot of good information hidden in financial data.[9]

Lastly, companies have to figure out how to move away from operating on the principle of the economics of scarcity. Google, for example, is a company that makes lots of money even though they give away a lot; they do this because they don't pay for the content they monetize. But even when they do pay, they realize that it's sometimes worthwhile to give it away. For example, Google entered into deals with Navtech and TeleAtlas in order to license data which it realized it needed mapping services. And yet Google Maps is making the information accessible for free. And because they provide free API(application programming interface) access, they've disintermediated the other guys and become the key mapping platform.

Challenges to Harnessing Collective Intelligence

There are, of course, challenges or obstacles to a company successfully harnessing collective intelligence. O'Reilly suggests that the primary challenge is that the first one in wins. You better be first into the market, as this then gives you the opportunity to keep improving. A natural monopoly can be based on the network effect. I is difficult to come from behind and topple the market leader. Many companies want to be the next Google or the next MySpace or Facebook. But you can't do that with incremental improvements. As O'Reilly noted recently in one of his blogs,10 in the early 1860s Emerson made this comment to a then-brash young Oliver Wendell Holmes: "When you strike at a king you must kill him."

A second challenge is that companies need to understand what Web 2.0 assets they already have. Web 2.0 is about building user-facing services driven by network effects databases.[11] A notable shortcoming is that many companies fail to take advantage of network effects in the data they already have. O'Reilly points out, for example, that there is an amazing network effect in e-mail communication, and yet this source of data is not mined.[12] Another example is credit card companies who have access to an incredible amount of information that could be used to build new user-facing services, such as a smart address book for the phone, but they are not pursuing it. A company such as Wesabe (in which O'Reilly is an investor) is building collective intelligence services based on bank and credit card data. The banks and credit card companies could have done this, but they haven't.

Because Web 2.0 and the core notion of collective intelligence are relatively recent concepts, how should people assess its strategic value for their organizations? O'Reilly argues that Web 2.0 is held to an unrealistically high standard: "Instead, people have to view Web 2.0 and collective intelligence in its proper context."[13] These aren't magic bullets that solve every problem, and collective intelligence has its downside—collective stupidity, collective cupidity, and the like. There are always people who will corrupt every system—but that doesn't mean the system is bad. For example, the fact that spam exists doesn't mean that e-mail is not good. People sometimes believe that if something is not perfect, then it is not any good. The Internet is a living system, so it gets sick just as we do. But then it tends to heal itself, more or less.

The Future of Web 2.0

What does the O'Reilly Radar see for the future of Web 2.0? By way of context, Dale Dougherty, a Web pioneer and O'Reilly VP, coined the phrase "Web 2.0" in 2003. O'Reilly's company held its first Web 2.0 conference in 2004. So the term has been around for only four years, even though the trends O'Reilly Media has been tracking go back to the very beginnings of the Web in 1991.

First, as far as the future of Web 2.0, O'Reilly sees more new sources of collective intelligence data. He believes that the data assembled will not be information developed consciously by people, but rather given as a byproduct of doing other things. GPS data is a good example, or location data detected by cell tower location. Jaiku is a great example of a mobile application that is using this data to build smarter presence information into a cell-phone address book.

Second, O'Reilly thinks companies will devise more ways to extract insight from that data. Companies will put out sensors of different kinds. For example, Microsoft's photosynth project is using collections of photographs, from various angles, to experiment with reconstructing 3-D images of places and physical objects. This is an unexpected application of collective intelligence. Did you ever think of your snapshots as part of the Internet's computer vision system?

Third, there will be more interfaces away from the personal computer (PC) model. There will be movement away from using the Web for communicating. For example, to look something up quickly, instead of doing a Web search, more people will be text messaging on mobile phones (via SMS) in order to get a quick response.

Fourth, O'Reilly believes that there will be more people liberating data. Marc Hedlund wrote about this idea in a blog on July 25, 2007, titled "Making the web into a banking platform"[18] Hedlund explained that opening up APIs and embracing the Web as a platform is a great way to empower the people using a company's service.

Lastly, peer-to-peer networking will continue to emerge as a major theme. O'Reilly believes that right now it is still a subterranean model. But it's going strong. And because it's one of the major architectural innovations in Internet content distribution, it's going to show up in more and more contexts.

The Role of O'Reilly and the Future of Web 2.0

Why is it important to have Web 2.0 summits and expos? O'Reilly's business started off as writing books to explain technical things in a clear way. He states that one line he tries to live by is he attributes to Edwin Schlossberg: "The skill of writing is to create a context in which other people can think."[15]

His company is in the business of putting on conferences. But, of course, it is more than that. As the company Website states, "We have an unshakeable belief in the power of information to spur innovation."[16] This is based on O'Reilly's realization when he started in Internet business that people care about ideas and not just products. So, he has found that he is often spreading ideas of what is coming, and then they sell products as part of that. O'Reilly recalls that, "We realized that early, when there were only a couple of hundred Websites in the world, that this was going to be a revolutionary change. Later on we were evangelists for open source."[17]

Bringing people together is a key way to shape the way people think about what's important. When O'Reilly Media did its first peer-to-peer conference in 2001, a conference that was in many ways the predecessor to Web 2.0, it surprised people by having keynotes not just on file sharing, but also on distributed computation (SetiAtHome) and Web services. They were trying to put file sharing in the broader context of the Internet as platform, rather than just the narrow framing of music and copyright. Eventually, they were able to establish the idea of the Internet as platform under the name Web 2.0.

Similarly, they have launched a recent project called "Maker Faire" to go along with their successful *Make* magazine; it is a county fair for geeks.[18] Dale Dougherty, the creator of the magazine and Faire, broadened the DIY category to show the common impulse that drives hackers and crafters. And so at the Faire, in one pavilion Dougherty had the "Swap-o-rama-rama," an event started by a woman in New York in which people swap clothes, and then remanufacture them on the spot, with sewing machines, silk screening, and so on, and then have a fashion show at day's end. In the next pavilion are a bunch of Linux geeks with their biodeisel-powered supercomputers made out of recycled PCs. Dougherty was able to give these people a new common identity as "Makers." O'Reilly explains that his company's approach is about meme engineering and how to see things differently. They are always looking at how to reframe categories. The skill of writing is to create a context in which other people can think, but that's also the skill of conference organizing.

Step 1
The Entrepreneurial Lens

$100 billion in company value was represented by the men and women who walked the stage at the Web 2.0 summit last October, most of them having risen to billionaire status within the first and still uncompleted decade of the 21st century. Of that total, $15 billion in value was represented by a shy 22-year-old who has been in the business for only three years. Mark Zuckerberg, the now-billionaire founder of Facebook.com, appeared at the summit dressed like a teenager, in a hoodie and flip-flops. While tentative for much of the interview, he sprang to life periodically when speaking about building what he calls the "social graph" on Facebook—a graph of the people and relationships that matter to an individual. His comments were subsequently referenced throughout the balance of the conference as those of a junior oracle.

And yet he was making wise decisions beyond his tender years. In May 2007, only six month earlier, in the face of Facebook's rumored $1 billion offer from Yahoo, *Fast Company* commented:

> Zuckerberg's college-kid style reinforces the doubts of those who see the decision to keep Facebook independent as a lapse in judgment. In less than two years, the two reigning Web 2.0 titans have sold out to major corporations: MySpace accepted $580 million to join News Corp. (NYSE:NWS), and YouTube took $1.5 billion from Google. Surely any smart entrepreneur would jump at a chance to piggyback on those deals.[1]

What a difference six months can make. By the time of the Web 2.0 summit in October 2007, Microsoft was desperate to get a sliver of his company—a mere 1.6 percent for $240 million—at a cost that would put the total value of the company at a whopping $15 billion.[2] What is happening in the new virtual marketplace?

Web 2.0 and the New Virtual Marketplace

Names of people and companies that would not have generated a sniff of attention at the start of the decade are being lionized by the end of it. A few years back a number of these billionaires were regular students in undergraduate and graduate programs, or mouse-pushers in Dilbert-like cubicles.

Is this a new era, or a repeat of the previous boom and bust cycle at the turn of the millenium? A *New York Times* article on the summit highlighted that Web 2.0 companies are awash in dollars. Moreover, Mary Meeker of Morgan Stanley Investment Bankers remarked at the summit that "high-level Web 2.0 trends are very compelling." John Cisco, chairman and CEO of Cisco Systems, predicts that Web 2.0, social networking, and online collaboration are going to usher in a new productivity boom.[3]

The fact is, this new virtual marketplace is now rising to the forefront. The memory of ill-advised investments is now being disassociated from the present offerings. The shakeout has happened, and now it's time to rebuild. The flagbearer of the new virtual marketplace is Google, a company that was actually birthed in the midst of the dot-com boom: It fought the urge to rush for easy money during that time and instead held on to build a colossal organization. At the heart of Google is a sound business model that has great potential to be leveraged.

After the dot-com bust in early 2001, the Internet sector began a downward slide. Financing was practically impossible. What had previously been a badge of honor—talking about "burn rate" and "attracting eyeballs" to Websites—fell into disrepute. And yet a few industry insiders kept plugging away in the computer-cum-internet industry. One such person was Tim

O'Reilly, a leading publisher of computer books. In 2005 he de-cided to organize a conference to dissipate the dismal wake of the dot-com disaster. He called this conference the Web 2.0 sum-mit, a term his organization coined to signify a practical and psychological break from the first incarnation of the Internet. Web 2.0 meant a number of things, but mainly highlighted an online progression from reading to participating, from thinking to acting, from individual to community, from contemplating to interacting. O'Reilly's conference, the 2005 Web 2.0 summit, ush-ered in the renaissance of the Internet.

The summits have since gathered momentum to the point at which they are an invitation-only, coveted event with a stel-lar cast of presenters. Three days of presentations and panel discussions parade the who's-who of the Internet universe, from the crown princes to the elder statesmen—this is an insiders' gathering with a lot of shop talk, telling people what's hot, what's not, who is in favor and who isn't, and the lingo and jargon of the movers and shakers in the field.

The ramifications of the summit are belied by the casual style of the proceedings. Most of the speakers are interviewed either individually or as part of a panel, and they are usually prodded into giving candid comments or explicitly declining to address certain questions. The interview style of the confer-ence hosts and moderators, Tim O'Reilly and John Battelle, is a combination of late-night talk show host and Larry King. While polite, the hosts are industry insiders who ask direct and perti-nent questions.

Speakers at the Web 2.0 summit appear from backstage, most not having the inclination to cavort with the masses. They fin-ish their slot and—like the interviewees on Letterman or Leno—disappear backstage again.

AS mentioned earlier, Facebook was one of the most praised Web 2.0 companies at the summit. A social networking site, it had opened itself up months earlier to application developers. This was a critical inflection point, after which Facebook's membership base increased exponentially. Another reason for Facebook's popularity at the summit was that many summit guests are industry insiders, the developers who are actually benefiting from Facebook. The conference also highlighted a few companies (such as iLike) that abandoned their own Websites and became solely Facebook applications, with great success. This inviting mentality reflects the ideals of Web 2.0—more open than closed, more cooperative than territorial, leaving something on the table rather than trying to take the table.

The Web 2.0 Summit and the Entrepreneur

The aroma of the summit is that everything is new, and cutting-edge, that we are collectively going where no one else has ventured before. It is an exercise in exploration. And, though the territory is uncharted, we have equipment to help navigate the path.

In my opinion, the best way to fully understand this new virtual marketplace is to tap into an entrepreneurial framework. There is a wealth of entrepreneurial knowledge that, when applied to the Web 2.0 environment, will significantly advance our understanding.

One puzzling aspect of the Web 2.0 summit and the comments of the leading lights was that there were ongoing superficial references to entrepreneurial concepts, but without adopting a comprehensive framework. Part of the problem may be that when the technology is so new and everyone is looking forward, no thought is given to an analytical framework based on tried and true principles. This is likely the result of an unrecognized bias that looking forward should focus only on technology, not on traditional "analytical frameworks." Conversely, I believe that although the technology is new, the tools for analysis are decidedly not. The following five entrepreneurial concepts alluded to at the Web 2.0 summit, but could have been discussed more fully.

First, people spoke of technology and its impact on the markets, but made no reference to the entrepreneurial context. Specifically, a number of presenters talked about innovation in the Web 2.0 space and mentioned "disruptive technologies," a term popularized by Clayton Christensen.[4] But the notion of disruption by way of technology goes back to Austrian economist Joseph Schumpeter, often hailed as one of the fathers of entrepreneurship. His seminal contribution was to analyze entrepreneurship as an economic force and speak of it in terms of "creative destruction."[5] (See Step #2, "Classic Insights on Innovation", page 76, for more information.)

Second, innovation was a popular term used throughout the summit. Rupert Murdoch, billionaire head of Fox Corp., emphasized, "Silicon Valley is a world center for innovation." Murdoch's purchase of MySpace, based out of Los Angeles, gave him a foothold in California. He stated his intention of migrating closer to the font of innovation in Silicon Valley. (This explained Rupert Murdoch's motivation to acquire MySpace—initially at a price of $580 million, which seemed ridiculous at the time. Ironically, by the 2007 Web 2.0 summit, the acquisition was rumored to be worth 20 times the initial purchase price.) Similarly, John Doerr, Kleiner Perkins, and a director of Google, praised the Google founders for their continual insistence on technical excellence, a sense of urgency, and the desire to build a great team. Then came the climax: "At Google," the director stated, "innovation is the lifeblood of everything we do."

Surprisingly, this talk of innovation was not linked to an entrepreneurial lens—and it must be. Entrepreneurship is at the heart of making innovation accessible, just as innovation is at the heart of entrepreneurship. We will explore this concept further in Step #2.

A third critical element at the heart of entrepreneurship is the life cycle of organizations, a topic that Web 2.0 company owners need to understand in order to succeed long-term. Sadly it was not even mentioned at the summit. The principle behind the life cycle is that entrepreneurial organizations must constantly be looking to adapt, or they will perish. To put it bluntly, some companies simply become dinosaurs, and others learn to change colors with the times. A case in point is CBS, one of the three major TV networks. How does a traditional TV station, once one of the three main sources of information being piped into American homes, maintain a position in an environment where the Internet is leading to a rapid disintegration of the station's original audience? Patrick Keane of CBS Interactive explained that CBS is making its programs available online, but in a different format. For example, CBS is still able to produce expensive, high-quality programs such as the wildly popular *CSI: Miami*, which attracts a worldwide following. In the online environment, CBS can make shorter segments available and thus expose the show to a new audience—strategically driving traffic back to the TV show. CBS interactive also realizes that Internet traffic is fickle; rather than seeking to attract traffic to its company's Web page, it will go where the traffic is. That's why CBS Interactive has five applications on Facebook. In short, CBS has tried to maintain its entrepreneurial culture even in the face of a mature organization. Along those lines, leading entrepreneurial consultant Larry Farrell notes that the life cycle of an organization involves four phases: start-up, high growth, plateau, and decline.

The Life Cycle of All Organizations

Entrepreneurial   Managerial
Practices   Practices

SOURCE: Larry Farrell, *Getting Entrepreneurial!*

The key for organizations is to maintain an entrepreneurial culture and sustain growth. As a result, larger corporations must strategize to maintain growth.

A fourth entrepreneurial principle was unknowingly cited throughout the conference: the importance of focusing on the customer. The entire nature of the Web 2.0 environment is oriented toward its customers, or "users"—soliciting participation, user-provided content, ease of use, and more. Because of its extensive options and its "surfing" capabilities, the Internet has become the indispensable and essential determiner of user-focused business: If a company doesn't please users, it won't last long. On the other hand, companies that deliver what users want will benefit from a rapid increase in visitors to their site. Larry Farrell, an internationally recognized entrepreneurship expert, writes, "The single most crucial vision all entrepreneurs must have is a clear picture of a specific set of customers who need and will pay for a specific set of products and services. Nothing could be more basic to the entrepreneur."[6] Farrell explains that a successful entrepreneur is almost always both a "product person" and a "customer person." Farrell recounts the story of Walt Disney, the "greatest product creator in the history of the entertainment business."[7] Farrell concludes, "The trick, then, is to become passionately expert on your own products and customers. After all, they are the two most important ideas in business."[8]

A fifth principle reflects the nature of entrepreneurship as one of the best levelers in the world—it is open to anyone of any background. This factor was evident at the summit, an indirect testament to the international allure and meritocracy of the Web. Many Canadians and Indian émigrés to the Valley participated in the summit's proceedings, and Mattias Miksche from Scandinavia, the CEO and cofounder of Stardoll.com, was in the spotlight for his booming start-up. In addition, Nokia from Finland was well represented, and the conference also recognized an Argentine entrepreneur for his success. This International collection of talent was not even commented upon, likely because it is so commonplace. Instead of catering to national boundaries, the internet lets the most effective technology or product—from whichever corner of the globe—win the race for market supremacy.

The Entrepreneurial Process

As the examples in the previous section demonstrate, an entrepreneurial perspective is necessary for a fuller understanding of the Web 2.0 company phenomenon. To help explain an entrepreneurial perspective, I draw on the insights of Jeff Timmons, a leading entrepreneurship educator I recently interviewed.[9] Timmons is a professor of entrepreneurship at Babson College, Wellesley, Mass., and a pioneer in the field of entrepreneurship education. Timmons defines entrepreneurship as "a way of thinking, reasoning, and acting that is opportunity-obsessed, holistic in approach, and leadership balanced."[10] Those who think in this way will recognize opportunities where other individuals see none.

How does someone with an entrepreneurial mind master the entrepreneurial process? Timmons states, "At the heart of the process is the creation and/or recognition of opportunities, followed by the will and the initiative to seize these opportunities."[11] In his perspective, a recognized opportunity without initiative is a tripod with two legs. The entrepreneurial process is the method by which an individual with an entrepreneurial mind is able to assess risks, distinguish ideas from viable opportunities, and gather resources to pursue this niche in the market.

What precisely does the entrepreneurial process involve? In general, ventures with a substantially higher success pattern are: (1) opportunity-driven; (2) creative and resource parsimonious; (3) guided by a lead entrepreneur and an entrepreneurial team; (4) examples of appropriate balance between these elements; (5) a good fit for the opportunity; and (6) integrated and holistic.

First, the process starts with an opportunity—not money, strategy, networks, a team, or the business plan.[12] In plain terms, no other factors are relevant until one finds an appropriate opportunity to pursue and determines a valid starting point. The opportunity should also receive support from investors. Then the size and scope of the opportunity will dictate the necessary amount of resources, the nature of the team, and the strategy required. Sadly, but worth noting, the vast majority of opportunities are not able to attract financial backing.

After an entrepreneur secures the initial opportunity, the process must control resources in a "parsimonious and creative" fashion. Sharing office space and equipment, swapping small bits of equity in the company for advice from key advisors, traveling on stand-by, and designing your own logos are ways to minimize cash outlays. Money is one necessary resource, but it should be supplemented by sources of information, professional advisors, and a range of industry relationships.

The most common misconception among inexperienced entrepreneurs is that nothing can be accomplished without money. Timmons reflects, "If you grabbed 100 people on the street at random and asked them, 'Does it take money to make money?' they would all say, 'Yes!'"[13] He goes on: "[Most people think] entrepreneurs who have a lot of money have a higher chance of success than those who don't. But you can dispel that as a myth," he observes, "because it has been erroneous, and just dead wrong, and backwards so many times. Get people to look at cases where you buy a $40 million business for a buck. It happens all the time."[14]

Timmons considers this delusion—that "money is the most important start-up ingredient"—so prevalent that he includes it among his list of the 15 main myths of entrepreneurship.[15] He has seen that not every opportunity requires money. Instead, the entrepreneurial process succeeds through creative use of *all* resources, which may include money, but are by no means limited to it. In other words, securing funding is not the single key to establishing a business.

After the first two considerations (the opportunity, followed by the creative, parsimonious use of resources), the third element of the entrepreneurial process is developing a team. A great entrepreneurial leader who stands alone can attain some level of success, but typically not enough to build an organization that achieves sustained growth. A company with a single leader is a commercial cult; if the entrepreneur leaves, the company (which exists independently in name, but not in fact) will simply implode. For obvious reasons, this is not the finely tuned organizational model investors prefer.

Thus, one entrepreneurial imperative is to demonstrate the existence of a team and system that can ride through difficult patches and replace key players along the way. As the popular saying goes, investors prefer a Grade-A team with a Grade-B idea over the reverse. The Grade-A team will figure out a way to make the business work, and will overcome the challenges of a sudden change in circumstance or direction.

Fourth, the venture must arrive quickly at a balance between the key elements of opportunity, resources, and team, and must properly determine where each element fits in the overall picture. For example, if a large opportunity has insufficient resources, the business is likely to fail. Similarly, if a team is too big for the opportunity, dissension will fester among the ranks. Thus, the entrepreneur needs to keep these three elements of the model in balance.

What about the "fit?" Timmons addresses this question by asking, "This is a fabulous opportunity, but for whom?"[16] The entrepreneurial process will only succeed if the opportunity, resources, and team fit the particular circumstances. People can only exploit an opportunity if they have the expertise to do so. Therefore investors in one country may forego opportunities in an emerging market, such as China, because they lack familiarity with the investment dynamics. The opportunity may have been a good one, but it was not an appropriate fit for the team and resources available.

Finally, an entrepreneur's approach to the process must be "integrated and holistic." An entrepreneur must integrate multiple factors to determine how an opportunity should be pursued. For example, ambiguity and uncertainty may exist in the external environment. Yet at the same time, internal decisions will affect the venture: The company requires funding, so it needs to satisfy the requirements and expectations of investors. In the midst of this swirl of considerations and uncertainties, the entrepreneur has to apply leadership, creativity, and good communication skills. Furthermore, Timmons emphasizes that an entrepreneur must do this in a holistic manner: Specifically, the entrepreneur must step back and assess each opportunity in light of all constituent factors. Timmons comments, "This integrated, holistic balance is at the heart of what we know about the entrepreneurial process and getting the odds in your favor."[17]

This general background of the entrepreneurial process provides a framework for the discussion of the "crowd-empowered entrepreneur," or "crowdpreneur."

The Rise of the Crowdpreneur

Crowd power is often treated as an interesting novelty, a way of experimenting as a dilettante with ways of attracting online traffic (users) to a site or enticing outsiders to provide gratuitous assistance. We are in the early days of crowd power and its true potential is only now being uncovered. There is much potential but relatively few examples of success.

So the question is, how can an entrepreneur tap into that market effectively, and what does a business gain from it? As I noted in the Introduction, I advance the term "crowdpreneur." The short definition is a "crowd-empowered entrepreneur." The long definition is: An individual or organization that uses the strategy of online crowd empowerment in its various forms (collective intelligence, mass collaboration, crowdsourcing, and others) in the pursuit of an entrepreneurial venture.

In other words, "crowdpreneur" is shorthand for applying entrepreneurial principles to this new area of collaboration in the Web 2.0 world.

How can we understand the role of a crowdpreneur in a practical sense? The focus of this book is not on establishing definitional boundaries or delving deeply into underlying trends, but rather to examine how an entrepreneur assess the current online arena to determine whether or not it holds worthwhile opportunities.

I discussed earlier the threads of crowd power, from "crowd clout" to its most popular term, "crowdsourcing." The definitions of the terms, including "crowdsourcing", vary among commentators and bloggers. Although Jeff Howe has provided a definition of crowdsourcing, other commentators use a variation of his original concept. For example, one blogger views crowdsourcing companies as simply those that "are addressing tasks previously performed by established business entities."[18] Because I cannot dispute what crowdsourcing should precisely entail, as it is Jeff Howe's term to define, I will instead focus on the various threads of crowd power from the perspective of the end goal of the launch of a new venture, which is the focus of this book. This approach is embedded in the definition of a crowdpreneur, which involved crowd power in the pursuit of an entrepreneurial venture.

I will explain the role of the crowdpreneur within the context of conventional strategic planning. Strategic planning is simply rational business thinking—a way to organize thoughts around the objectives of a firm. In strategic planning there are three key phases: (1) formulation, (2) implementation, and (3) evaluation. The starting point in the formulation phase is to determine the vision and mission of a company. The vision drives at "What do we wish to become?" and the mission relates to "How does it do its business?" At this instance we can determine the importance of crowd power.

Is crowd power one of the company's key components? If so, then crowd power is likely at the core of its business model, which is at the heart of the strategic planning process. The objective of the corporation is to generate revenue in order to sustain itself and to achieve other objectives. To pursue its mission, the company comes up with objectives. The objectives are then implemented through strategies. If crowd power is at the core of its business model, then one of its core strategies will relate to crowd power. The company uses various tools (involving all the functional departments of the firm) to implement that strategy. So, if its core strategy involves developing crowd power, then various departments of the firm—such as the marketing department—actually use crowdsourcing to fulfill its objectives.

One of the key aspects of my crowdpreneurial approach is that the actions of the firm are tied either to the firm's mission or to some specific outcome. In that sense, then, crowdsourcing becomes a strategy. If, on the other hand, utilizing the crowd is simply a new and interesting concept that the firm attempts to integrate, then it is simply a tool for implementation—and may not be as effective.

We can understand crowdsourcing in relation to its objectives within the firm—it is either a core strategy or a tool of one or more strategies. Thus, "crowdpreneurial companies" are those that use crowdsourcing as a core strategy. Other companies simply use crowdsourcing concepts as a peripheral tool of strategy, and are not considered crowdpreneurial overall. In simple terms, if utilizing the crowd is not tied in closely to the business model of a firm, then it is simply an interesting concept, a theoretical idea, but not a viable business strategy.

My interpretation is that a crowdpreneurial strategy can apply at two levels of the strategic planning process: (1) in the formulation of strategies, and (2) in the implementation of strategies.

First, crowd-empowered tools apply to the phase of strategy formulation—this is the stage at which the internal and external environments are being scanned and understood in terms of important trends. Crowd-related tools, to the extent that they focus on the means of receiving consumer (that is, crowd) feedback, then form part of the "formulation" process. The crowd's input can help establish long-term and annual objectives for the firm. In essence, the crowd addresses the question, "What does the firm wish to achieve?" These objectives are then pursued through strategies: "How do we achieve the objectives?" Once this formulation has been finalized, the firm moves to implementation. At this stage it puts into practice the objectives identified by the crowd, gathering the resources of the firm to implement the chosen strategy. Where a crowdpreneurial approach occurs in the formulation of strategies it is then a core component of the company's business model (in other words, the company is dependent on the crowd for generating revenue).

But what if a company wants to actually create itself around a crowd-powered product or service? Let's suppose a company wants to develop a news-gathering system for "citizen journalists"—everyday citizens who write their own news articles based on the parameters established by the company. The essence of the company is to develop and publish news online. The objective of the company, then, may be to create a vibrant and growing online community of devoted users, with the means of generating revenue to be determined at a later date. This company's strategy would be to make the crowd-empowering model effective. Thus the tools required to implement the strategy relate to community building, appeal of the site, ease of use, ability to motivate users, and so on. An example of this is *www.nowpublic.com*, a crowd-powered news Website.

A second aspect of crowdpreneurship is that it is used as a tool of the implantation of a strategy. In this instance, the company is not dependent on the input of the crowd and is simply using the power of the crowd to help implement one of its strategies.

To use a practical example, a shoe company may set the objective of selling more shoes. The long-term objective may be to sell $10 million worth of shoes in the next five years. The annual objective for the coming year may to be to sell $1.5 million worth of shoes. The shoe company may pursue one or more strategies. Specifically, it may choose between market penetration, market development, and product development. Let's say the company wants to pursue market development—to sell to people in new markets who don't have ready access to, or knowledge of, its shoes. A tool to implement this strategy would be to launch a Website geared toward those people. An additional tool, however, would be to have a Website built on a crowdsourcing model, which is more engaging and interactive for customers. Therefore the crowdsourcing Website is a more useful tool for implementing the Web strategy, which in turn generates more sales. At the same time, depending upon the nature of the interactivity (that is, feedback to the company on its products, marketing strategies, plans for expansion, and so on), the information is useful not for the implementation of the particular strategy (that is, a good Website to increase sales), but rather it is useful to help the company in its planning. In the previous scenario, crowdsourcing is a tool that makes a particular strategy more effective. In addition, the feedback it generates from users may improve or inspire future strategies. This innovative shoe company actually exists—it is called Fluevog Shoes.

Of course, by providing the previously mentioned definition of a crowdpreneurial approach, various companies are not included—even though they would otherwise be viewed as being encompassed under the various threads of crowd power. For example, are Google and Amazon crowdpreneurial companies? No. Are they crowdsourcing companies? Yes. Google, through its algorithms used for searching, does give search results based on people's preferences as revealed through hits on pages. This component of crowd feedback helps make one of Google's strategies—to be a dominant force in the search market—work effectively. Google can be viewed as the leading crowdsourcing company in the world. However, it is difficult to call Google a crowdpreneurial company because it is primarily successful through its search engine and targeted advertising. Yet Google still has a very compelling business model. It integrates the feedback from the crowd, and in that sense it adopts some of the principles of crowd-empowerment. Similarly, Amazon provides feedback to consumers based on recommendations in other buyers' profiles. The company is getting basic consumer information from the crowd, but it is not getting the crowd to pitch in directly. Amazon falls into the same camp as Google in this case: Both companies utilize the crowd effectively, but are not crowdpreneurial companies at their cores.

Succeeding as a Crowdpreneur in the New Virtual Marketplace

The approach of the crowdpreneur is a natural evolution of the present "crowd" chatter as it relates to the nuances of the process and a fascination with the novelty of connecting people online. A crowdpreneurial approach focuses on one critical aspect of crowd power: What is the business objective to be achieved by the firm? I am defining crowd-powered strategies in relation to the value of the end goal.

An entrepreneur should assess the value of a crowdpreneurial strategy in relation to his or her company and its goals. What can a crowdpreneurial strategy be? Would it be a core or non-core aspect of the company's strategic planning process?

In light of the recent interest in Web 2.0 companies and the generally high valuations they have received, there is a fascination with the potential of involving the crowd. Everyone has an abstract sense that it will work and it will pay dividends—but the challenge comes in how one translates that feeling into reality. Realistically, the companies reaping the benefits of the Web 2.0 buzz have achieved returns for shareholders as a result of their membership or visitor base rathe than as a result their ability to generate revenue.

As mentioned previously, crowdpreneurship is a fusion of crowd empowerment and entrepreneurship. Therefore the five-step process in this book follows a standard approach to any entrepreneurial opportunity, applied to the field of Web 2.0 and crowd-powered strategies. The five steps are as follows: (1) Your company must adopt an entrepreneurial lens (this is the framework for constructing an approach), (2) your company must use innovation as a measuring stick for opportunities, (3) you must conduct a feasibility analysis of the opportunity, (4) you must develop an effective business model, and (5) you must organize how you will finance your company. Following these steps will heighten your chances of success in the new virtual marketplace.

Step 1 Recap

- ✓ Web 2.0 developments are redefining the Internet, from small start-ups to the retooling of large international firms.
- ✓ The annual Web 2.0 summit in Silicon Valley presents leading Web 2.0 information.
- ✓ A gap in current Web 2.0 discussions is the lack of an entrepreneurial framework for analysis.
- ✓ There are five specific aspects of an entrepreneurial framework that can be used to better understand Web 2.0:
  - ⇨ disruptive technologies
  - ⇨ the nature of innovation
  - ⇨ organizational life cycles
  - ⇨ customer/product focus
  - ⇨ the equalizer effect
- ✓ A crowdpreneur is an individual focused on using crowd power in a strategic planning model, whether as a core strategy or as a supplemental in the implementation of a strategy, in the pursuit of a corporation's goals.
- ✓ The key to succeeding as a crowdpreneur in the new virtual marketplace is to focus on executing the five steps of the crowdpreneur, culminating in the successful growth and financing of a new venture.

COMPANY PROFILE

Cambrian House and
the Crowdpreneurial Approach

NOTE: This Company Profile provides a brief introduction to Cambrian House. Various aspects of the company and its operations are covered in the interview with its founder, Mike Sikorsky (page 190 and throughout the book).

Mike Sikorsky is a wild-eyed, spiky-haired business revolutionary who is a pioneer in the Web 2.0 world of crowdsourcing specifically and crowd power generally. I first met Sikorsky when we presented on the same panel at a hi-tech gathering in March 2007. Sikorsky delivered his message with his customary rapid-fire delivery that had earned best-of-show honors at several investment conferences. His crowdsourcing-dedicated company is based in Calgary, AB, Canada, but has taken a leadership position worldwide.

Sikorsky's company, Cambrian House (*www.cambrianhouse .com*), is unquestionably the leading crowdpreneurial company in the market today. The power of the crowd is at the core of its business—without the crowd it would not exist. Most importantly, it is not treating crowd power as an adjunct to its business (that is, reducing research and development costs); rather they are focused on the practical applications of developing a viable business model. It is the #1 crowdpreneurial company in the Web 2.0 world.

The seed of the company began in late 2005 when Sikorsky was raising money for his proposed venture. At that time, although the term "crowdsourcing" had not yet been coined, the notion of "wisdom of the crowd" was gaining currency. He decided upon the name "Cambrian House" in reference to "the

Cambrian explosion." James Surowiecki makes this paleonto-logical reference in *Wisdom of the Crowds*. Jeff Bezos "com-pared the Internet boom to the Cambrian explosion, which was the period in evolutionary history that saw the birth and extinction of more species than any other period."[1] The "house" part of Cambrian House is based on the notion that there is a financial discipline, a methodology, as a result of this Cambrian period. In other words, software companies are similar because of the diversity of inventory that begins and eventually dies away if it can't survive.[2] The objective of Cambrian House is to use "the wisdom of the crowds to find the best new business ideas and to fine-tune those ideas for mass distribution."[3] So-cieties contain a number of budding entrepreneurs, and Sikorksy noted that they often don't have the money or con-tacts to develop or market their ideas; his company's plan was to unite people to create and market those ideas and to share in the profits.

The original phrase adopted by Cambrian House was the "architecture of participation," which the company explained was the phrase that "has come to define one of the key elements of what's been called Web 2.0, which describes the collection of companies, technologies, and projects that are designed around the culture and economies of openness."[4] Then, a few months later when Jeff Howe created the term "crowdsourcing," Cam-brian House realized that this was the buzzword of the future, and latched on to it. Cambrian House changed its tagline to "crowdsourced software." Sikorsky was staking his future and his company on the crowdsourcing wave. The company explained that, "we feel Cambrian House is ideally positioned to catch and ride this wave. To date, we know of no other commercial software provider that is attempting to capture this mind share land grab.

We want to be the first and the best on the commercial crowd-sourced software scene."[5] This was an early turning point for the company: to recognize the term and adapt. Their response: "Ramped up to own it."[6]

The vision of the company is that "crowdsourcing is an essential part of the business landscape."[7] This is more a statement or proclamation than a vision statement. The mission of Cambrian House is to create a platform that "enables people and businesses to harness the wisdom and participation of the crowds—for commerce."[8] The mission of the company, how it does its business, is presumably to build that platform around commercial undertakings. As noted previously in Step 1, for a company to be crowdpreneurial, its approach to crowd power can be at the core of formulation or instead a tool of implementation. With Cambrian House, crowd power is at the very core of the business.

Cambrian House has positioned itself at the forefront of the commercial application of crowdsourcing. It describes itself as "the home for a community of people with broad talents and interests that come together to create products that the world wants, markets those products, and shares in the profits."[9] The premise is explained on the Website as follows:

> Many people have great ideas but not enough money or contacts to develop or market them. Millions of people around the world have great talents but only the option of working for an hourly wage, and many times not even using their real skills and interests. Cambrian House aims to unite those people and empower them to create and market those ideas and to share in the profits. Modestly stated, Cambrian House is bringing in a revolution in how business is done![10]

Cambrianhouse.com launched on June 26, and within 10 days had immediate traction: 1,126 community members, an average of 100 new community members per day, 403 submitted ideas, 59,000 visits (approx. 6,000 visits per day), and 182,000 page views.[11]

Product Offering and Solution

The company's Executive Summary explains that the product of the company is to offer a platform for anyone to start a venture. The individual can submit an idea and market it in the community. People start a project, advertise, and assign tasks to manage their project. Next, they can host a Website on the Cambrian House platform. If other community members get involved, they can grant equity or money to other members in exchange for services. Any fees payable to Cambrian House are contingent upon the success of the venture. Finally, there may be an opportunity to microfund the venture through an internal public-offerings forum. The wisdom of the crowd is important in determining which projects from the community get support. This was the initial plan of Cambrian House; while the overall methodology remained consistent, the details of the process would be fine-tuned through time.

One of the challenges for any crowd-related site, which relies on the involvement of members, is to ensure their motivation for ongoing participation. Cambrian House positions itself to attract two groups. First, the site seeks "venture creators" (entrepreneurs)—those with an idea who are not able to commercialize it due to lack of funds and other resources. Second, the site needs "venture participants" who are prepared to contribute sweat equity in the hope of some return. Of course, the site will not be successful unless both groups of individuals are motivated. Cambrian House developed a form of commerce based on both dollars and recognition. Contributors can get paid in "Cambros," the unit of currency at Cambrian House (1 Cambro = US $1). In addition, there are "glory points" that go to active members in recognition of submitting and voting on ideas, starting a business, or posting in forums.

Community Owned

One of the issues that Sikorsky wanted to address was to give members some actual ownership in the company. He recognized that the problem with online social communities and user-generated content is that members don't share in the financial success, yet their content and loyalty is what made the company valuable.[12] On April 17, 2007, Cambrian House launched their "Community Owned" initiative: They became the first Web 2.0 company to share equity and revenue with its community. They set aside 1 percent of the revenue and 1 percent equity in the company for members. This share allocation is provided to community members who accept a "member share" when they sign up. By accepting the member share, they become part of a co-op governed by a board of community members who decide at annual co-op general meetings how to distribute shares and money by giving to active members and/or investing in businesses in Cambrian House.

The Branches of Cambrian House

Cambrian House has four "branches," or divisions. First, there is the Cambrian House platform for sourcing ideas and regulating crowdsourced behavior. The company defines this as an individual branch because it is a specific potential profit center. The other three branches, although they owe their birth to the

Cambrian House platform, are distinct products and revenue streams: Gwabs, which is a video game; Prezzle, an online gift-wrapping service; and greedyorneedy.com (formerly the Robinhood Fund).

Branch #1—Cambrian House Platform

Since inception, the chief value in the company has been the creation and development of its operating platform. The operating platform allows the crowdsourcing to occur. The company has continued to refine the platform based on crowd feedback since inception, and CH 1.0 has given way to CH 2.0. The most significant development is yet to come, however. After its Annual General Meeting in July 2007, Cambrian House announced that it was working on "CH 3.0," which it began referring to as its "Crowdsourcing Operating System" (also referred to by the company as "Chaordix"). The objective was to build a crowdsourcing operating system whereby crowds can lay their foundations, build community, and share/collaborate with other crowds. The company made the comparison to Manhattan with the crowds as buildings of knowledge workers sharing and creating, with commerce baked into everything they do.[14] The leadership position developed by the company throughout slightly more than a year garnered the interest of other players who wanted to develop crowdsourcing applications. The company noted that, "We're already working with beta networks who have confirmed their interest in being the first crowds!"[15] The objective is that CH 3.0 will create a "socially aware" operating system "that allows individuals and firms to create, share, collect, and monetize the wisdom of crowds."[16] CH 3.0 is intended to create an online ecosystem that supports productivity and innovation—it will be a place where knowledge workers can host their professional profiles, and where new and existing crowds can live. CH 3.0 will become a separate source of revenue for Cambrian House, apart from specific products that have been spun out of the community.

Branch #2—Prezzle

A second project launched by Cambrian House is the "Prezzle" (*www.prezzle.com*): a virtual and interactive gift box to wrap a gift certificate (from Amazon, for example) in an emailed package. The company developed and started testing Version 1.0 of Prezzle in March 2006, and it was launched in April 2006.[17] Here's how it works. The process involves three simple steps for customers. First, they choose a particular type of Prezzle at a "wrapping station." Second, they send a gift certificate from a specified list of retailers (such as Amazon.com, iTunes, and so on). Finally, they customize the greeting card the recipient will receive with an individual message, a hint for the gift, and the opening date. Once this is done, the customer simply signs out using the PayPal payment system. The recipient is then sent an e-mail containing a link to the virtual and interactive gift box.

Prezzle is an online service that deals only with the transaction of online gift certificates. It does not handle physical property from third parties. Unlike "free" e-cards that have become vehicles for spyware and spam, Prezzle is a real service that allows individuals to send online gift certificates in style. The goal of Prezzle is to earn loyalty by providing a great experience for both sender and receiver. No software is required, as Prezzle is a Web-based service using Macromedia Flash technology. The sender only needs a Web browser and e-mail address to send and receive Prezzles. Currently Prezzle only supports wrapping online gift certificates and not physical gifts.

Branch #3—Robinhood Fund/Greedy or Needy

A third project launched by Cambrian House integrates many of the features required for a successful crowdsourcing site. In July 2006, Cambrian House began to develop the concept for "The World's First Web 2.0 Wishing Well." The new Website allowed any individual to submit a wish and let the crowd vote on the wish they thought should be granted.[18] Originally under the name Robinhood Fund, the site is now known as *www.greedyorneedy.com*. It provides a vehicle for giving modest donations to individual causes. Recent $100 postings include requests for "Back rent and car payment" or a "Memorial Garden in Honor of My Son." As the site explains, "It's a chance to grant everyday wishes to everyday people. Present your case to the world. You just might get your wish."

The site explains how to participate in Greedy or Needy. Individuals join to get access to all of the site's features. They can then make a wish: submissions are entirely free of charge. Members can participate in the community, make friends, send messages, have fun with surveys and games, and promote their favorite wishes. They are able to rate up the wishes they would like to support or make a direct Paypal donation to someone's cause.

Each submitted wish competes against other wishes for views in either "Greedy" or "Needy" categories. Users directly support wishes simply by viewing them. However, they can also rate a wish while viewing it, to let others know which ones are compelling and which can be avoided. Wishes are granted per category according to the highest number of votes. The site contacts participants with top wishes to give them their funds.

The site is a straightforward concept and has all the key elements of a successful crowdsourcing site. The crowd decides what happens. A person simply submits his or her wish and the Internet community decides if it should be granted. Top wishes in each category receive the maximum current funding amount. Winners are selected through the user voting process. Users vote 1 to 5 stars on a wish (There is no zero-star rating). The wish with the most Wish Points at the end of each week wins. If viewers think a wish should not receive continued community support, they can "rate it down," thereby encouraging others to skip the wish. Interestingly, the value of each individual's input is not the same. How much each user has participated in the site also affects the weight of his or her vote: Someone with full participation (100 percent), will have his or her vote count twice as much as a user with 0 percent participation. A person gains participation points by performing various actions, including rating wishes, taking polls, leaving comments, and more (each person has a participation meter). And, whether or not an individual's wish is granted, the individual will receive any money donated directly to his or her cause (via Paypal).

Branch #4—Gwabs

A fourth branch that has been launched throught the Cambrian House platform is a video game known as "Gwabs" (*www.gwabs.com*). Gwabs is the first desktop-to-desktop combat game in which you can fight your friends in real time over the Internet. Participants use their "skills, weapons, and intellect to survive this Gwab-vs.-Gwab battle royale." Players can take on their friends or Gwabs community members through the Battle Manager portal. They build up their Gwablet points and climb the ranks of the worldwide leaderboard to become the most powerful and respected Gwabs fighter. Players can customize their characters by choosing unique colors and tattoos;

they can also choose from more than 10 different weapons for each character, such as swords, nunchuckus, or metal hand spikes. In addition, they can interface with Skype to trash, talk their opponents during battles, and they can challenge anyone within the Gwabs worldwide network for immediate desktop-to-desktop battles. The purpose of the game is to defeat one's opponent by winning 2 out of 3 rounds; each round lasts for 60 seconds, or until a character loses its entire lifeline.

The niche for the game is that it is a quick but action-packed gamer break for those who need to get their fix but don't have time for more complicated games. Cambrian House has been accepting pre-orders since the site was first launched.

The company has also been looking to develop Gwabs on a large scale. In August 2007, HotHead Games invited Cambrian House to Vancouver to meet with Piranha Studios and Atomic Cartoons. The goal was to partner with a professional game development studio and Gemini award–winning cartoon studio to push Gwabs past the finish line. The partnership is moving forward, and three members of the Gwabs team will work side-by-side with Piranha to develop the complete closed-beta version.[19] The game should be released in 2008.

Step 2

Opportunities
Through Innovation

The preceding profile introduced Cambrian House, which describes itself as "The Home of Crowdsourcing." How did Sikorsky come up with the idea of applying crowdsourcing to software development? His story illustrates how an idea takes shape and then evolves into an opportunity through applying innovative thinking.

As a kid, Sikorsky was an avid video game fan. By the age of 13 he had started developing software. As he grew up he maintained an ongoing interest in providing his own open source contributions. Prior to starting Cambrian House he had been involved in four start-up ventures. In light of his interest in software and his experience with open source contributions, he became intrigued with evolving Internet technologies and their effect on collective behavior. He began reading books such as *Wisdom of the Crowds* and *The World Is Flat*.[1] He recognized that open source provided great business opportunities, but he knew from his own experience that the way that it was being monetized and the way companies were giving incentives to participants was terrible. There was a basic problem: "People would figure out a way to build great computer software, but then companies would move backward in time by imposing an outdated corporate structure for compensation. It made no sense."[2] He wanted to figure out how to develop new incentives and a corporate structure that would make sense for the community. Cambrian House is an early stage of that concept. He also realized that involving crowd power as a core strategy could have practical benefits. Sikorsky explained that, "I had an earlier product company where I was basically generating inventory— and hoping for sales. I know that for my software company, we guessed at what we wanted to do and then we guessed what the marketplace would want. Then we started to build the product.

But, when we go to sell it, no one wanted it."[3] Sikorsky realized that crowd power could help his new company avoid those problems.

Separating Ideas and Opportunities

In the Web 2.0 world, as in any new and growing sector, there is an excitement about the possibilities of new technology. How can existing businesses take advantage of new developments? And, from a different perspective, can a business originate and grow from an Internet base?

Step #2 to succeed in the new virtual marketplace is the pursuit of opportunities in the context of innovation. Innovation is at the heart of entrepreneurship, and the Web 2.0 world is ripe with innovative entrepreneurial opportunities. Yet a crowdpreneur must, like any entrepreneur, distinguish carefully between an idea and an opportunity. Investors often view ideas as a bus: there will be another one in 10 minutes! In other words, ideas are possibilities—but an opportunity is an idea that is worth executing and can be successfully realized.

What is the difference between an idea and an opportunity? An idea is merely a thought, a concept, or a notion of some proposed undertaking that may or may not work. It is a potential course of action that has not been seriously examined. An opportunity, on the other hand, is an idea that has merit and is worth pursuing in the business sector. In other words, an opportunity is a confluence of circumstances that creates a need for a new product, service, or business. One writer notes that an opportunity has four essential qualities: It is (1) attractive, (2) durable, (3) timely, and (4) anchored in a product, service, or business that creates or adds value for its buyer or end user.[4]

How, then, can an entrepreneur identify an opportunity? The range of opportunities discovered will be balanced by the inclinations of the entrepreneur and the nature of the particular environment. On the one hand, a person who is obsessed with starting an entrepreneurial venture will be predisposed to see opportunities, whereas others might not. This is sometimes referred to as an "opportunity obsession."[5] This person may travel in circles with other entrepreneurs and may have a wide range of contacts looking to invest and participate in opportunities.

An entrepreneur should be an astute observer of societal trends, thinking of what is to come rather than of what has already been done. To that extent, the entrepreneur's ability to predict future business behavior is important. Behavior is shaped by many forces: Economic trends involve the state of the economy, fluctuating interest rates, the amount of disposable income, employment rates, and consumer spending patterns. Social forces can involve interest in recreational properties, a desire to have pets, or the number of dual-income households. Demographic trends, examined later in more detail, relate to generational patterns. Lastly, an important factor, and one that is central to our discussion, is technological trends.

Classic Insights on Innovation

It is important to understand the context of innovation as one of the critical steps in succeeding in any venture, including in the new virtual marketplace. As mentioned earlier, a starting point for any discussion of the entrepreneurship thoughout the last 100 years must include the classic insights of Joseph Schumpeter. One biographer *notes,* "Schumpeter's signature legacy is his insight that innovation in the form of creative destruction is *the* driving force not only of capitalism but of material progress in general."[6] As with the insights of many prescient thinkers, his progressive developments are now accepted as widespread truths.

Schumpeter first used the now commonlycited term "creative destruction" in 1942 to describe how innovative capitalist products and methods continually displace old ones.[7] Interestingly, his description of the entrepreneurial environment seems to ring true in the Web 2.0 world: "Old concerns and established industries, whether or not directly attacked, still live in the perennial gale. Situations emerge in the process of creative destruction in which many firms may have to perish that nevertheless would be able to live on vigorously and usefully if they could weather a particular storm."[8] In other words, entrepreneurship is a dynamic force that destroys certain industries, namely those that will not adapt, while it gives birth to new companies.

Schumpeter was also a chief proponent and propagator of the word "entrepreneur," which appeared in the 1934 English edition of his *Theory of Economic Development*. Schumpeter draws a sharp distinction between inventors and entrepreneurs, and between inventions and innovations: "The making of the invention and the carrying out of the corresponding innovation are, economically and sociologically, two entirely different things."[9] In short, Schumpeter emphasized innovation as being at the heart of entrepreneurship and as being part of the inevitable upheaval that is an outgrowth of the process.

The link between innovation and entrepreneurship was strengthened by Peter F. Drucker, often referred to during his lifetime (1909–2005) as the world's leading management thinker. Drucker, however, was also a leading entrepreneurship expert. His 1985 book, *Innovation and Entrepreneurship,* is one of the leading books in the field. It analyzes the nature of the entrepreneurial process and provides a philosophical understanding; comparatively, most other books are survey types, providing an overview of the mechanics of the process.

Drucker's definition of entrepreneurship has a specific focus: innovation. Thus he distinguishes between entrepreneurial businesses, which involve innovation, and other small businesses, which do not. For example, a person who develops and markets a new product is an entrepreneur, whereas the typical corner grocer is not. Likewise, a restaurant franchisee may not be an entrepreneur, while an independent restaurant owner may be.

In other words, entrepreneurs focus on innovation, and innovation is rooted in creating change and endowing existing resources with new wealth. Entrepreneurs view change as the source of opportunity in the marketplace—they embrace change rather than avoiding it. For non-entrepreneurs, this way of thinking is an aberration. Drucker writes that an entrepreneur continually "searches for change, responds to it, and exploits it as an opportunity."[10] This means doing something different, which is the realm of innovation, rather than simply excelling at something that is already being done. The latter may be profitable, but falls into the realm of increased productivity through operational improvements.

The next step for aspiring entrepreneurs, according to Drucker, is to continually practice a process called *systematic innovation* by identifying and pursuing opportunities and recognizing that change creates an opportunity for entrepreneurs to generate personal wealth, which indirectly, provide value to the overall economy. Drucker remarks, "Innovation is the specific instrument of entrepreneurship. It is the act that endows resources with a new capacity to create wealth. Innovation, indeed, creates a resource."[11] The created resource—as this is not a zero-sum game—provides value in the marketplace by deploying unproductive resources for more productive purposes.

Drucker affirms that because entrepreneurship is not a mere personality trait, individuals can learn the innovation process.

Obviously, increasing one's ability to innovate does not guarantee financial success, but it will provide more opportunities for consideration. Drucker posits, "Systematic innovation, therefore, consists in the purposeful and organized search for changes, and in the systematic analysis of the opportunities such changes might offer for economic and social innovation."[12] Rather than presenting a broad definition that defies meaningful analysis, Drucker's explanation demystifies the process of entrepreneurship. As well, his specific focus provides a clear starting point for developing one's own entrepreneurship practice.

Going further, Drucker identifies seven sources of innovative opportunity. Four sources lie within a business, and the other three are due to changes outside the enterprise or industry. The first source is the "unexpected" occurrence: the unexpected success, the unexpected failure, or the unexpected outside event. Drucker recounts the well-known tale of Ray Kroc—not the founder of McDonald's Restaurants, but the person who built the company into the colossus that it is today, with its globally recognizable Golden Arches and its famous cast of cartoon characters. Ray Kroc was selling milkshake machines to small-scale restaurants when he noticed that one of his customers, the McDonald Brothers Restaurant, bought an unusually large number of the appliances. This unexpected event led him to discover that the restaurant had an overwhelming amount of customers due to its streamlined menu, low prices, and fast service. In response, he eventually bought out the brothers and built his burger empire.

According to Drucker, a second source of innovative opportunity may be an "incongruity" between reality as it *actually is* and reality as it is *assumed to be*, or *should be*.[13] In the mid-1980s, when Drucker wrote *Innovation and Entrepreneurship*,

O.M. Scott & Co. was the leader among U.S. producers of lawn-care products (grass seed, fertilizer, and pesticides). It then became a subsidiary of a larger corporation called ITT. Basically, the company became a leader in the industry because of a simple mechanical gadget called a "spreader," a small, lightweight wheelbarrow with holes that allowed the proper quantities of Scott's products to pass through in an even flow. Prior to the Scott Spreader, no supplier of lawn-care products gave the customer a tool to control the process.[14] Yet without such a tool, there was a total incongruity in the logic of the process; there was no way to control the amount of fertilizer dispensed.[15]

A third source of innovation within the enterprise is innovation based on a process need, a restatement of the notion that "necessity is the mother of invention." As an example, Drucker cites the development of photography. In the 1870s, photographic processes required heavy and fragile glass plates, which had to be lugged around and treated with great care. The plates themselves required an equally heavy camera, and a long preparation time before one could take a picture.[16] In the 1880s, George Eastman, the founder of Kodak, replaced the heavy glass plates with cellulose film of negligible weight, and designed a lightweight camera around the film. Within 10 years, Kodak was the world leader in photography.[17] Interestingly, at the turn of this century, the postlude of continuing technological developments in photography—namely, the invention and popularity of digital photography—has created serious challenges for film companies such as Kodak. No less than in the late 1800s, the companies that recognized change, and thus capitalized on opportunity, now claim leadership in the field today.

Drucker's fourth and final source of innovative opportunity within the enterprise is changes in industry structure or market structure that catch most people unaware.[18] Drucker mentions differentiation within the car industry, where brand names for vehicles strategically carve out niches in the market. A vehicle has long ceased to be merely a means of transportation; now it is a status symbol and a reflection of one's personality. The phrase "You are what you drive," despite its facileness, is the mantra for many consumers. For example, a Rolls Royce automobile, the world's most expensive car, is fit for royalty—and others who spend royally. A BMW sports car is attractive to the up-and-coming executives, and the Mercedes-Benz sedan is respectable and reliable luxury on wheels.

As the market changes due to fluctuating preferences and buying power, new niches arise. One can look back to the mass arrival of Japanese cars in America in the 1980s, when consumers turned their backs on poorly built, fuel-inefficient American cars and emptied their wallets for reliable, well-built Japanese models. This shift in the market caught most of Detroit unaware, as did the more recent shift to hybrid vehicles (which happened first in the United States when Toyota introduced the Prius).

In addition to these four sources of innovative opportunity within a business, Drucker makes note of three changes outside the enterprise that create sources of innovative opportunity. The first is shifting demographic trends—including changes in population size, composition, employment, educational status, and income. Popular age-defining terms such as Baby Boomers, Baby Busters, and Generation Xers are designations that connote various opportunities as these groups move through their life cycles. Drucker explains that the success of Club Med in the travel and resort business stems from its capitalization on "demographic changes," specifically the growing number of wealthy and well-educated young people with working-class family backgrounds.[19]

Club Med tapped into this opportunity, recognizing that the individuals in its demographic focus are "ready-made customers for a new and 'exotic' version of the old teenage hangout."[20] Club Med continues to exploit demographic trends, having recently diversified locations for singles, couples, and families.

Another source of innovative opportunity is a change in perception, mood, or meaning. Drucker recounts how people previously ate based on income and class; thus, ordinary people "ate" and the rich "dined."[21] Today's trend has been toward "feeding," however, which is simply a matter of getting edible food in the fastest and simplest manner possible. Customer satisfaction depends on speed of delivery rather than quality of product. How many people will patiently wait in a McDonald's line-up for more than a minute? Very few, indeed. Yet no one expects McDonald's to deliver an exceptional product. Successful food service companies have been those who understood and exploited this attitude.

The third source of innovation opportunity outside the enterprise is the "superstar" of entrepreneurship: new knowledge, both scientific and non-scientific.[22] Drucker describes the features of this source: First, it has the longest lead time of all innovations. Specifically, scientific discoveries, such as those in biotechnology and pharmaceuticals, require regulatory approvals that involve a tedious completion process. Secondly, new knowledge is usually based on several pieces of prior knowledge converging, not all of which are technological or scientific, and not all of the knowledge necessary for innovation is available. Therefore, one must conduct a careful analysis of all the factors required to perfect the product. Following that process, a company must develop this new knowledge for commercialization, and that company must identify its strategic position in relation to its competitors.

Finally, in order to successfully execute the commercialization, the company must aim for dominance—because the innovation based on new knowledge will probably have plenty of competition. The innovator must get it right the first time.

To summarize, Drucker provides classic insights on innovation and entrepreneurship that reflect his life experience though the 20th century. He highlights seven sources of innovative opportunity: four within the enterprise, and the remaining three outside the enterprise. His discussion of these opportunities reflects a systematic and purposeful approach to identifying, understanding, and applying the heart of entrepreneurship, which is innovation. What are some of the current insights on innovation?

Current Insights on Innovation

One of the leading thinkers on innovation, and routinely cited in the high-tech community, is Harvard Business School Professor Clayton Christensen. Christensen is the author of two seminal books: *The Innovator's Dilemma: The Revolutionary Book That Will Change the Way You Do Business* (1997) and *The Innovator's Solution: Creating and Sustaining Successful Growth* (2003). As noted in the Introduction, a number of presenters at the 2007 Web 2.0 summit referred to "disruptive technologies." What does this mean?

In *The Innovator's Dilemma*, Christensen addresses a key issue: Why do good companies fail to see opportunities? He comes to the counterintuitive conclusion that "*good* management" is the driving force behind the failure of large firms such as IBM, Sears, and Xerox. The firms followed all the right rules: They listened to their customers, they invested in technological improvements, they studied market trends, and they "systematically allocated investment capital to innovations that promised the best returns"—but those exact actions prevented them from engaging in the entrepreneurial risk and innovation that characterized their competitors.[23] The implication of this approach is that some of the widely accepted principles of good management are only situationally appropriate.

How, then, should people deal with this dilemma? Christensen presents his "principles of disruptive innovation," which are rules that managers can use to judge when the widely accepted principles of good management should be followed and when alternate principles are appropriate.[24] The principles are intended to apply to a wide range of businesses, high tech or low. In his view, technology is "the processes" that organize "labor, capital, materials, and information" to create increasingly valuable services or products.[25] As a result, technology is not only advancement in engineering or manufacturing; rather, it can be the improvement of processes spanning everything from marketing to management. Innovation, therefore, is "a change in one of these technologies."[26]

Thus his "innovator's dilemma" is that "the logical, competent decisions of management that are critical to the success of their companies are also the reasons why they lose their positions of leadership."[27]

How can businesses manage the principles of disruptive innovation? If managers can understand and harness these forces, rather than fight them, they can in fact succeed spectacularly when confronted with disruptive technological change.[28] Christensen lists five principles of disruptive innovation in order to enable managers to understand the situation. Principle 1 is that "Companies depend on Customers and Investors for Resources." A company must have a cost structure that will allow profitability at the low margins, which is characteristic of most disruptive technologies. Principle 2 is that "Small Markets Don't Solve the Growth Needs of Large Companies." Christensen writes about the first-mover advantage as a significant factor in the competitive struggle for success.[29] This is the strategy of Cambrian House, a leading crowdsourcing company (see Company Profile on page 63) that is blazing a new trail in terms of crowdsourcing in the field of software. It is the first mover.

Principle 3 states, "Markets That Don't Exist Can't Be Analyzed." Christensen explains that larger, managerial firms prefer to pursue avenues that involve predictability and analysis. After all, managers are taught to *manage* resources prudently.[30] Along those lines, managers are often unprepared for disruptive technologies that entail higher risk—so they tend to avoid them. However, the strongest first-mover advantages exist in these high-risk fields, and thus the smaller, entrepreneurial companies are better positioned to take advantage of these new opportunities. Christensen refers to this conundrum as the innovator's dilemma.[31]

Christensen's Principle 4 is that "An Organization's Capabilities Define its Disabilities." An organization has capabilities with respect to processes and values. Principle 5 is that "Technology Supply May Not Equal Market Demand." Christensen believes disruptive technologies may start small, but they quickly become mainstream. At that point they become strong competitors against well-known preexisting products.[32]

How does a manager or entrepreneur cope with disruptive technologies and maintain a spirit of innovation? Christensen suggests that managers uproot their managerial assumptions and search for "unanticipated successes."[33] As Mike Tippett of NowPublic notes (see his Company Profile on page 124), customers may use products differently than expected, and a good company will learn to adapt accordingly. Christensen also states, "discoveries often come by watching how people use products, rather than by listening to what they say."[34] By being flexible and adapting to unexpected opportunities, companies can keep the spirit of innovation alive.

Christensen refers approvingly to the "discovery-driven planning process."[35] The originators of this phrase, "discovery-driven planning," are two well-respected entrepreneurship professors, Rita McGrath of Columbia University and Ian McMillan of the University of Pennsylvania. I previously interviewed McGrath on the topic, and also have gleaned additional insights from the book she coauthored with McMillan titled *The Entrepreneurial Mindset*.[36] McGrath and McMillan pose the following question: "How do you plan and manage an initiative whose direction and outcomes are not yet known?"[37] McGrath's response is "discovery-driven planning," an approach that encourages entrepreneurs' inclinations to act, and teaches subsequent readjustment through careful attention to a strategy's evolution. Because one cannot determine the strategy in advance (and an attempt to do so may actually be counterproductive), this approach places greater emphasis on a process of reflection and analysis. Discovery-driven planning is much different from conventional planning, which focuses on trying to envision the end result and then securing corporate allocation of resources to achieve those relatively unsubstantiated goals. McGrath teaches that, in the context of uncertainty, conventional planning is suspect at best and dangerous at worst.[38]

In contrast, McGrath establishes six disciplines of discovery-driven planning. whereas conventional planning is rooted in past experience and precedent, discovery-driven planning focuses on entirely new patterns. With that in mind, the six disciplines of the discovery-driven planning framework balance traditional attention to costs and cash flow with the cutting-edge input of creativity and new ideas. McGrath's intended outcome, then, is "real options reasoning," which seeks to minimize initial costs until a venture actually demonstrates returns.[39]

The six disciplines are as follows:

1. **Framing:** According to McGrath, any new initiative that does not have the potential for "substantial, quantifiable impact" is not worth pursuing. The goal of framing is to clearly specify the "unit of business," which McGrath defines as "the product or service that actually triggers a revenue-generating event."[40] This unit of business, which varies from a billable hour for lawyers to a policy for life-insurance agents, defines the business model.

2. **Competitive Market Reality Specification:** One must conduct the planning process within the bounds of a realistic appraisal of the particular market. A company should bear in mind the range of competitive challenges—namely the effect of new companies, or the threat of existing companies that will reallocate resources. Though in-depth knowledge is not necessary at this stage, the entrepreneur has to grasp a project's "benchmark parameters" for success in a competitive environment, as well as the market range required to sustain a product's profitability.[41] This discipline may quickly eliminate unrealistic ideas.

3. **Specification of Deliverables:** An entrepreneur must translate his or her broad strategy into daily operating activities in order for the idea to become a reality. Deliverables are defined in relation to the frame of the business model in the context of a

discovery-driven plan. McGrath points out four reasons why deliverables should be specified. First, the process converts a lofty strategy to the specific production goals and abilities of team members. Second, the specific deliverables provide a focus for competence-creation: For example, collecting a certain percentage of funds from delinquent customers may require telephone skills, a certain number of calls per staff, and a minimum number of staff. Third, this step exposes any of the planners' fallacious assumptions by confronting their ideas with operational reality—is the venture truly feasible? Specifically, salespeople can quickly judge if customers are likely to buy the new product, and at what price, regardless of what management expects to happen. Fourth, the more closely deliverables are intertwined with the actual needs of customers, the more difficult it will be for a competitor to break that bond.[42]

4. **Assumptions-Testing:** In a conventional plan, people test the end result; in discovery-driven planning, however, testing assumptions is a continual process. A list of assumptions accompanies each deliverable and its operating requirements. As the execution procedure progresses, owners test these assumptions against reality with the objective of gaining as much actual knowledge as possible without incurring large expenses.[43]

5. **Managing to Milestones:** McGrath defines milestones as "critical, identifiable points in time at which key assumptions are tested." This discipline is, of course, related to testing assumptions at frequent junctures

in the discovery-driven process. The core concept is that an individual plans as far ahead as current information will sensibly allow; then he or she stops and reassesses the assumptions, after which he or she manages to the next milestone.[44] Throughout the process, the individual maps and re-charts the major milestones that are likely to occur. For a manufacturing procedure, such milestones typically include concept test, model development, focus group test, prototype, market test, pilot plant, and full-scale plant initial run.[45] One challenge in this process is to stage a sequence of events that "minimize cash burn and corporate expectations" yet engage the entrepreneur in critical research.[46] The advantage of the discovery-driven approach is that company directors are changing strategies to conform to continual feedback, as opposed to ascribing to expectations established prior to the start of the program, when knowledge was merely speculative.

6. **Parsimony:** The last discipline proposed by McGrath is parsimony—creatively finding ways to minimize the costs of the planning process. Faulty assumptions, whether with regard to production costs or acceptable consumer price levels, can be very expensive. Again, McGrath encourages companies to commit minimal resources until assumptions have been tested. She advises people to "spend their imagination" before they reach for their wallets.[47]

The discovery-driven planning process ties in well with the notion of today's online communities and the premium put on user-generated interfaces and dialogic interaction with clients.

New managers need to "directly create knowledge about new customers and new applications through discovery-driven expeditions into the marketplace."[48]

Where are the opportunities for smaller, new ventures that are the focus of this book? Christensen concludes that small emerging companies have an advantage: They are often able to take entrepreneurial risks that the larger, established organizations cannot justify taking.[49] In the context of Web 2.0 technologies, some larger firms are adapting, but many of the success stories in the sector are from smaller, innovative firms that do not have allegiance to a previously formed administrative structure.

Individual Versus User-Centered Innovation

The classic and recent insights on innovation provide context as to how innovation occurs within organizations. But how does innovation occur in today's Web 2.0 world? I referenced the concept of open innovation earlier in the Introduction. Can a group of people—a crowd—be innovative, or is that the domain of the legendary sole genius?

The stereotypical image of the entrepreneur is that innovations are the product of genius, developed in isolation— whether a shack in the woods or on a mountaintop. The reality is that such is seldom the case. Most inventions, including Edison's light bulb or William Darrow's game of Monopoly, were the result of teamwork and incremental improvement through an extended period of time. This has important implications for an entrepreneur.

In *Group Genius : The Creative Power of Collaboration*, Keith Sawyer outlines the seven key characteristics of effective creative teams: (1) innovation emerges over time, (2) successful collaborative teams practice deep listening, (3) team members build on their collaborators' ideas, (4) only afterwards does the meaning of each idea become clear, (5) surprising questions emerge, (6) innovation is inefficient, and (7) innovation emerges from the bottom up.[50] Sawyer's analysis is that innovation is generally a team-based process and that, in fact, the team yields superior results to an individual-centered approach.

Sawyer speaks of "webs" of collaborators, whether or not they are in an online environment, and this is not to be confused with the World Wide Web. Sawyer summarizes the five key features of a collaborative network: (1) each innovation builds incrementally on a long history of prior innovations, (2) a successful innovation is a combination of many small sparks, (3) in collaborative webs, there is frequent interaction among teams, (4) in collaborative webs, multiple discoveries are common, and (5) no one company can own the Web.[51]

The breakthrough of the new virtual marketplace is that innovative ideas can be derived from a group of people. In other words, the crowd comes up with an innovative solution and the entrepreneur delivers that solution back to the crowd. The entrepreneur is no longer the sole "inventor"; rather, he or she is one step in a process of collaborative development and delivery.

Why is this mass innovation occurring now? With rising levels of education and the increasing availability of technology, many people have access to greater expertise, tools, and information. There is also a growing desire for self-expression among Gen Yers, who often take the Internet for granted and (as detailed in the Introduction) embrace the medium as a means of community-building. The Internet has become a widely used global resource, and is thus a method of communicating with the largest human network in existence. User-centered innovation exploits the Internet as a tool for social and entrepreneurial improvement.

For companies that can master this process, crowd involvement will become an insurmountable competitive advantage. A small but gifted research team will have trouble competing with a distributed network of passionate contributors to a cause. This type of innovative process is embedded in an open source approach, in which a number of contributors all perfect a project.

How does this work in a practical sense? William Taylor and Polly LaBarre in *Mavericks at Work* explain how to put collaboration, or what they refer to as "open source innovation," to work for you and your company. Taylor and LaBarre speak of this concept as "open-minding your business." First, they advise companies to "keep the focus narrow and tightly defined."[52] Second, "keep broadening the range of participants."[53] Third, "keep it fun."[54] Taylor and LaBarre caution, "Innovation is serious business, but if you're working to tap the brainpower of grassroots volunteers and outside-the-mainstream contributors, then you have to work to keep your open source project colorful, dramatic, and energetic."[55] Fourth, they warn not to "keep all the benefits to yourself." This is one of the issues that crowd-related companies are presently sorting out: how to motivate and appropriately reward contributors. Taylor and LaBarre explain, "If you expect strangers (or even employees and colleagues) to share their best ideas with you, then don't be surprised when they expect something in return. It can be money, it can be recognition, but more often than not what draws people into open-source projects is the chance to interact with the best people in the field."[56] Fifth, Taylor and LaBarre advise, "keep challenging yourself to be more open to new ideas and new ways of leading."[57] A critical part of the process is to be transparent and remain innovative.

Another valuable perspective on innovation in the Web 2.0 world is that of Douglas Rushkoff, author of *Get Back in the Box*. He views open collaboration as an important strategy that enhances the core competency of a firm and creates a tie to innovation. This approach will lead to revolutionizing industries worldwide. It "requires a willingness to challenge and even rewrite the most accepted tenets underlying our industries, and to invite our employees and even our customers to engage in that process with us. This is the real meaning of open source" and the surest path to a sustained culture of 'innovation.'[58] Rushkoff views the open source movement as revolutionary in attitude: "Open source is more than a computer-programming ethos. It's the impetus to an approach toward work and life that makes secrets and protectionism obsolete, and opens the floodgates of innovation on an unprecedented scale."[59] In short, open source creates innovative opportunities for those companies willing to embark on the journey. Rushkoff points out, "Open source may be a new business model, but it's also a well-tested, even ancient, approach to innovation."[60] The least innovative companies are the ones most threatened by collaboration. Their state of mind is reflected in various practices. For example, "Companies that engage in anti-competitive (or, most accurately, anti-collaborative) practices are usually so heavily steeped in a scarcity model that they put more effort in protecting the past than building the future."[61] Rushkoff also notes, "There's no shame in opening up innovation to others, or even to one's customers. Accepting ideas from the bottom up is not an indication of weakness, but a sign of strength."[62] One clear example of Rushkoff's point is Fluevog Shoes (see Company Profile on page 156), which has benefited enormously from collaborating with its customer base online.

The Social Web as a
Platform for Innovation

Collaborative innovation in the Web 2.0 world cannot occur without a crowd. The group of people—or crowd—forms online because of social interaction. Why did we move from Web 1.0 and the display of information to Web 2.0 and socializing online?

Social networks have, of course, always existed—the question is merely the places where they manifest themselves. Robert D. Putnam, author of *Bowling Alone:The Collapse and Revival of American Community* (2000), provides a fascinating context as to the reasons that the Web 2.0 world has integrated online communities.

Putnam describes how community groups began to fade in America in the last several decades of the 20th century.[63] His book addresses the notion of "social capital," which refers to "connections among individuals," as well as "social networks and the norms of reciprocity and trustworthiness that arise from them."[64] He explained the dominant theme of this book as follows: "For the first two-thirds of the [20th] century, a powerful tide bore Americans into ever deeper engagement in the life of their communities, but a few decades ago—silently, without warning—that tide reversed and we were overtaken by a treacherous rip current. Without at first noticing, we have been pulled apart from one another and from our communities over the last third of the century."[65]

This death of community helps to explain the rise of social networks on the Internet as a way to fill the void. People want to connect and be in community, but the traditional means—such as bowling leagues and Rotary service clubs—have lost their luster. Instead, online networks are all the rage. Putnam foretells the speed of this adaptation: "The speed of diffusion of this new technology has been substantially greater than that of almost any other consumer technology in history—rivaled only by television. To go from 1 percent market penetration to 75 percent required nearly seven decades for the telephone; for Internet access the equivalent passage will require little more than seven years."[66] Similar to virtually all technological innovations, this one has caught on among younger generations. The Internet as a unifying tool has become a platform for collaborative innovation as a result of its ubiquity—particularly among the young.

This nexus of people online around a particular passion or platform is part of what is commonly referred to as the "social web." The social aspects of being online are infiltrating society. In particular, as was discussed in the "Generational Divide" in the Introduction, are now quite engrained in Gen Yers' lifestyles. The trend of the social web picked up momentum in October 2003 when a pioneering company called Friendster.com began to change the way people communicate with one another, connecting people to people rather than to other Websites. As *Inc.* magazine (June 2007) noted, "The beauty of Friendster was its exhaustively complete network. Every time a homepage loaded, Friendster's servers calculated a single user's connection to other users within four degrees of separation, which could mean hundreds of thousands of individuals."

Friendster was not able to take full advantage of its opportunities, however, and others jumped in. Intermix built a copy-cat site in 2003 called *MySpace.com*, which replaced Friendster as the focus of online socializing for many people. Other social utilities emerged in the marketplace as well. A prominent and now ubiquitous site is *www.facebook.com*, a social utility that connects groups. From Mark Zuckerberg's humble start in 2004, the site has blossomed. Current numbers of site participants are staggering: with 47,000 college, high school, employee, and regional networks, 600 million searches, and more than 30 billion page views per month, Facebook is the sixth most trafficked site on the Web.

People join social networking sites for a variety of reasons: to meet people, entertain themselves, to learn something new, and to influence others.[67] There are several factors that influence how often members will visit a site: the amount of activity among members; the importance of the shared interest among members (that is, a hobby or business); the flexibility allowed members to control release of profile information (is it simply an e-mail address, or a more extensive profile?); and notification through an invitation from a contact or random discover of the site.

Step 2 Recap

- ✓ An idea is not necessarily an opportunity.
- ✓ An opportunity typically uses innovative ideas to produce something new, different, and desirable in the marketplace.
- ✓ The very nature of innovation is changing: What was once the domain of inventors and their corporations is now being offered up to the crowd.
- ✓ Today's innovation can prosper from the successful use of the crowd, which is accessible through Web 2.0.
- ✓ The Web is not only a place to connect socially, but it is evolving to energize the crowd to apply its power to various tasks of collaboration and innovation.

Feature

An Interview With Jeff Howe, Crowdsourcing Gure (By telephone August 31, 2007)

Jeff Howe is a writer for *Wired Magazine* who wrote a pivotal article in the June 2006 issue titled, "The Rise of Crowdsourcing." The article and the term he coined—"crowdsourcing"—resonated with many people. A buzzword was born. He is also author of a forthcoming book on crowdsourcing.

Richard Goossen: What is crowdsourcing?

Jeff Howe: As I explain on my blog,[1] I use two definitions for crowdsourcing. The "White Paper Version": Crowdsourcing is the act of taking a job traditionally performed by a designated agent (usually an employee) and outsourcing it to an undefined, generally large group of people in the form of an open call. The "Soundbyte Version": The application of open source principles to fields outside of software.

RG: What is the core of the definition of crowdsourcing?

JH: You have a job that was once performed by someone and you put it out to a large undefined group of people. The operative term is "undefined"; in other words, the call goes out to a crowd of unknown people.

At the same time, to work effectively, this crowd of unknown people must be within a relevant network. The call must go out within an "intelligent network" in order to get the right input. For example, putting out a particular call in primetime TV will be pointless since 99.9 percent of the people will likely have no idea what you are talking about.

When contrasted with TV, we can see why the Internet is a great tool for crowdsourcing. The Internet is a "many to many" environment: Many calls can go out to many intelligent networks. On the other hand, the TV networks operate on the principle of "one to many": one program for everyone.

RG: Why does a definition of crowdsourcing matter?

JH: I think it is important to build boundaries around the term "crowdsourcing." Any time there is a new field there is a proliferation of new words used to describe the new ideas. That's well and good, but it also impedes the progress of the development of the field, simply because it sows misunderstanding and imprecision.

RG: Becaus you were the person who coined the term, how are you trying to maintain the meaning you originally intended?

JH: The term "crowdsourcing" was picked up so quickly by the online and mainstream media that it was difficult to keep a clear definition of its meaning. I don't ultimately have control over how the word is used, but to the extent that I have some influence I will work in the service of clarity. The definition of "crowdsourcing" currently on Wikipedia is my definition, but it can be changed. And, of course, I want to have the term stay consistent with its originally intended meaning.

Within the next year or so (when my crowdsourcing book comes out) this will help in the process of defining the term so that we can continue talking about the concept.

One of my pet peeves is that, in the Web 2.0 world, there are many people who are guilty of using terms, including "crowdsourcing", without any sort of rigor. I think we will have to work together and decide what we mean by various terms. While I have a fairly strict definition of crowdsourcing, a lot fits under that umbrella.

RG: Is crowdsourcing evolutionary or revolutionary?

JH: A bit of both. Crowdsourcing is not a new concept, but the Internet has made the difference. For example, in 1714 the British government wanted to figure out how to measure longitudes. They offered a longitude prize (£10,000–£20,000 depending upon the precision of the device) to anyone who could help. Then, sure enough, some carpenter up in Yorkshire figured out the calculation. This fellow, John Harrison, devised a marine chronometer. He said you simply have to build a really complicated clock that will figure it out. He eventually got his prize. That's crowdsourcing, and you find forms of it throughout the ages. But it was only recently with current technology that it became a more efficacious means of solving problems.

RG: What is the relationship between a community network and crowdsourcing?

JH: If you have an established community, then I think crowdsourcing makes a lot of sense. However, you can't just create crowdsourcing in a vacuum. You can't simply think of crowdsourcing as a matter of, "I have a job and I'll just give it to these people to do it." Companies have to understand that people are going to have to get something out of it beyond payment, especially in relation to the community context.

RG: Why do people participate in crowdsourcing?

JH: People generally participate because they want to impress their friends, or, like an open source group of people, they all have a common expertise, and so they are going to collaborate together.

Generally what I am seeing as I do research for my crowdsourcing book is that financial rewards are lesser, or marginal, incentives. People are more interested in learning something, having fun, or it makes them look cool. People are just as self-motivated as they have always been, and I don't think we are uncovering some new strain of altruism. I think that social scientists and business people have failed to realize the complex motivations of people

RG: Is this not a big challenge, for companies to deal with people who have varied motivations?

JH: It is not mystical; there are ways to appeal to people's motivations. I think Cambrian House does a good job of giving recognition.[2] Often money is used as a signifier for reputation. Even though the amount given by the company to contributors may be modest and may end up being a very, very small part of their entire income, it may still be enough to make members feel like they won a prize. There are ways to create these incentives. In the beginning, I think these incentives bubbled up just as a byproduct of communities. As crowdsourcing matures, then companies will figure out how to do this more deliberately.

In most cases, you are dealing with mass participation, so you need some way of sorting out the room, and if you have some reputation system set up then you have some way of incentivizing people. Often communities don't simply want to incentivize people but they genuinely want to figure out who is talented and who is not.

RG: How can a company make crowdsourcing work?

JH: There are a lot of principles related to crowdsourcing to make it work, that are not part of crowdsourcing. Most importantly, a company must have immense respect for customers: Make what customers want, not what you think they want.

RG: What should companies beware of when using crowdsourcing?

JH: First, companies need to realize that a basic rule of crowdsourcing is that 90 percent of any given submissions are not going to be worthwhile. This is Sturgeon's Law, named after science fiction writer Ted Sturgeon, who said, "Ninety percent of everything is crud" at the World Science Fiction Convention in Philadelphia in 1953.[3] Second, a company needs to understand the dynamics of group intelligence, which is central to crowdsourcing. In other words, how do groups of people actually work together? There are sometimes strong incentives within groups of people to hide information or to selectively present information.

RG: Who are some leading crowdsourcing companies?

JH: The top crowdsourcing company of them all is Google; it is crowdsourcing in all it does. One example is PageRank, which is based on an algorithm that obtains relevance data for Web pages from the Web links placed by Internet users. IBM is brilliant; it has made a big turnaround during the last decade or so. IBM has a beta site called Many Eyes[4] where you can see your data visualizations and multiple people can access them for a collaborative experience. Procter & Gamble is increasingly using crowdsourcing; it posts a variety of challenging scientific problems on InnoCentive's Website.[5]

RG: What are key success factors for companies that want to use crowdsourcing?

JH:

1. Companies that inspire passion will do well, and they will have a leg up with respect to crowdsourcing.

2. Companies should view crowdsourcing as a way of attracting the widest possible range of creative input on problems; by contrast, crowdsourcing is not primarily a labor-saving device (although there may be an increasing incentive for third-world providers of services who may be motivated by the money that can be provided).

3. The money offered to contributors is largely symbolic; a more important motivation is that the company recognizes the value of that particular individual's contribution.

4. Companies need to think of crowdsourcing from a longer-term perspective; the process is one of organic growth rather than something that will help them in the next couple of quarters.

Step 3
Feasibility Analysis
of the Opportunity

Cofounders Jake Nickel and Jacob DeHart came up with the concept of Threadless in 2000.[1] They started it as a side project until 2003 when they moved in to a 4,300-square-foot office. At that time, they were hiring part-timers to help them run the business. A year later, in 2004, they had hired eight full-time staff memebers. In 2005, the company moved to a 10,000-square-foot office and employed 15 staff members. One year later, the company office was 25,000 square feet and the founders had secured an investment from Insight Venture Partners.

What does the company do? Threadless uses crowd power as a core strategy to match and connect unique T-shirt designers with buyers. They are clearly a crowdpreneurial company. Out of this simple idea has sprung a business that collects $6.2 million in revenue a year and shows no signs of slowing down. By combining entrepreneurial innovation with Web 2.0 principles, Threadless created a consumer-centered product offering that encourages repeat interaction with the company.

How did Threadless decide what shirts to make? They asked the people. In this manner, Threadless also uses crowd power as a tool in the implementation of its strategy. Threadless devoted minimal resources to the business until consumer demand justified their expansion. The growth of the company eliminated the product feasibility risk, although the risks of organizational resources and industry dynamics are still a factor.

Users of the site not only shop, but they also rate current designs, submit T-shirt ideas, and upload photos of themselves wearing their favorite shirts. Jeffrey Kalmikoff, the chief creative officer of Threadless, described the company's approach: "In a nutshell, our business is based on the idea of 'customer co-creation' or 'user innovation' or 'crowdsourcing,' or whatever the next buzzword for it is…. Threadless is an ongoing, online T-shirt design competition. The designer of each winning T-shirt receives $2,000 in cash and prizes: $1,500 cash, a $300 gift certificate to Threadless, and a membership in the 12-club, a monthly subscription-based line of limited-edition tees."[2]

Kalmikoff continues, "Our community is [diverse and sometimes difficult], like any community. We make changes to the site, and some people aren't happy.... The key is to stay transparent and let the community know what's going on. As long as people feel like they have a sense of ownership and still have a say (which they do) in what goes on, we can do anything. If we wanted to sell to Target [for example], we would engage our users, have a discussion, and decide on what's right for the community."[3] The spirit of Threadless has the hallmarks of a Web 2.0 company in terms of disposition and motivation. Kalmikoff remarks, "It's a simple concept: When people tell you what they want, you give it to them. It's totally open—you can't have secrets, executives, and a bunch of bureaucratic levels in a top-down business hierarchy. It has to be completely transparent."[4] Doesn't this type of corporate development make a mockery of the conventional approach to a feasibility analysis?

Product/Service Feasibility Analysis

The experience of Threadless is an example of how crowd power can minimize the risks of launching a new venture. In the case of Threadless, the opportunity was developed in response to crowd feedback. In some ways this is parallel to any business that simply responds to user feedback to gradually expand its offerings and invest more time and resources in doing so. However, the Web 2.0 environment facilitates and reduces the expenses of garnering crowd feedback. Is the Threadless example a model for the start-up of new ventures generally? No. It is, however, an example of how crowdsourcing can alter the nature of the feasibility analysis required when launching a new venture. This chapter reviews how to conduct a feasibility analysis for the launch of a crowdpreneurial company, and then draw conclusions as to how the conventional feasibility approach can be modified.

A feasibility analysis is the process of determining if an idea is viable. An entrepreneur needs to devote a certain amount of time and energy to a proposed idea to make an informed decision about whether or not to proceed with it. Every venture requires a certain amount of resources. Perhaps professional advisors need to be engaged for their accounting and legal opinions. Or the entrepreneur may need to purchase a research or industry report to understand the dynamics of a particular business. In addition, an entrepreneur can do a focus-group study to establish, especially in a start-up venture, if there will be a sufficient number of customers.

A standard approach is to test the concepts underlying a business. In other words, a company may give a preliminary description of the product or service to prospective customers to gauge customer interest, desirability, and purchase intent. The company does this to confirm that the underlying premise of the product or service idea resonates with the potential buyer. Further, the testing process will help refine the idea. The proposed customers can provide their feedback on the concept. In addition, a survey of potential customers will provide some indication as to the estimated sales of the product.

A well-designed concept test, usually called a "concept statement," is similar to an "executive summary." The concept statement includes a description of the product or service being offered, the intended target market, the benefits of the product or service, a description of how the product will be positioned relative to similar ones in the market, and a description of how the product or service will be sold and distributed.[5]

In the case of Threadless, they have, in essence, an online focus group providing ongoing feedback—at no cost. Further, transparency is an important aspect of building an active and engaged community online. This approach then makes available a range of information and documentation to the crowd for their input that would mirror what is typically found in concept statements.

Industry/Market Feasibility Analysis

So you've conducted a financial analysis for your idea, and the prospects are in your favor. What's next? Find out all you can about the industry in which your idea will have to thrive.

Key questions arise when addressing any industry. Is the industry accessible? How many competitors can enter the fray, and how easily? Are there greater barriers than simply hiring good people and finding money to allocate to problems? Does the industry contain ripe or underserved markets for innovation? Can any positions in the industry avoid some negative attributes of the industry as a whole? What are the industry nuances and no-no's?

In addition to offering an excellent product or service that is difficult to replicate, companies rooted in discovery-driven planning must be able to refine and fortify their competitive advantages as they move forward. Is that possible in the Web 2.0 industry? The Internet environment features ongoing changes with respect to everything from new hardware to new online concepts. People continually look for the next great advancement, and they are unusually open to new ideas.

In terms of positioning a company in the Web 2.0 world, founders must be aware of some lingering detritus from the dot-com bust of 2001. Certain clichés and catchphrases conjure negative images of the past. Mike Sikorsky of Cambrian House, for example, is reluctant to use the word "incubator" for his company because the term smacks of the dot-com era, when financiers would establish inexperienced founders to promote and raise money for flimsy projects that eventually deflated the economy.

You also must ask a series of venture-specific questions about your prospective industry.[6] First, is the industry a realistic place for this new venture? You must carefully consider the particular niche identified. With regard to the Web 2.0 industry, ongoing Internet research seems to continually source new competitors for any planned venture. Almost every search yields a variety of "hits," a process that can be frustrating for enthusiastic inventors who realize that someone else has already developed their ideas.

But, with competitors and potential competitors in mind, can you be more profitable than others in the industry? Though you may think that is possible, profitability is not always easy to execute. In fact, it seems that a learning curve for most new ventures just can't be avoided. Perhaps you've created a unique business model that is difficult to duplicate—this issue will be examined in detail in Step 4. However, I will note now that uniqueness is more probable in the execution and appeal of a brand name than in the technology itself.

One important aspect of assessing the potential of the Web 2.0 industry is to put it into the context of different industry *types* and their respective opportunities. The Web 2.0 world is an "emerging industry." In this industry type, standard operating procedures have not yet been developed, and there are typically greater opportunities for the "first mover." Emerging industries are also characterized by high levels of uncertainty, fewer barriers to entry, and no established patterns of rivalry.[7] Another sector that the Web 2.0 field fits into is "fragmented industries," wherein a large number of firms of approximately equal size compete for customers. The primary opportunity in this case is for leaders who initiate a "roll up" or consolidation strategy, and thus achieve economies of scale. In contrast, "mature industries" are the opposite of the Web 2.0 world. They experience slow or no increase in demand, repeat instead of new customers, and limited product innovation. Related to this, "declining industries" experience a reduction in demand—and for obvious reasons, entrepreneurs generally avoid this sector.

I noted earlier that the Web 2.0 world values transparency. This assists companies in gathering "competitive intelligence"— information ethically gleaned by a firm about its competitors. Competitive intelligence is available through a variety of avenues: attending conferences and trade shows; reading industry-related books, magazines and Websites; talking to customers about what motivates them to buy your product instead of your competitors' products; purchasing competitors' products to understand them; and studying competitors' Websites.[8]

In addition to determining whether or not a product or service itself has market appeal, an entrepreneur needs to analyze the market in general. Both factors are equally important. Not only must the product have appeal, but there also needs to be a sufficient market environment in which to launch the product.

There are three primary issues. First, are you getting involved in a worthwhile industry? Industries vary considerably in terms of growth rates and profit margins. For example, a number

of years ago, I advised a client who was in the computer hardware and distribution business. The business was based in North
America and imported hardware through a major manufacturer
in Korea. Its gross margins were 10 to 12 percent and its net
income was 2 to 3 precent. It needed to generate a huge amount
of volume in order to be successful. In addition, a single bad
debt with a retailer in North America could cripple the business. Software development companies, on the other hand, can
have significantly better margins. Once the initial costs of research
and development are recouped, which is no small matter, the net
income for the company can be between 20 and 30 percent.

Also, what are the growth rates in the industry? Of course
the appeal of Web 2.0 crowd power companies is that there is
incredible potential for growth. Forecasts for the coming years
are that the Web 2.0 functionality will replace outmoded knowledge management systems. The reason is that application programming interfaces and social networking tools facilitate
bottom-up contributions, whereas previous knowledge management systems were top-down tools that forced users to
conform. In today's environment, users deploy "tagging" (at-
taching descriptive labels to Web content), which lets communities create their own "taxonomies" (hierarchical classifications
of related items)—sometimes called "folksonomies" (folksonomy
is the process of collaborative categorization through tagging, a
process made popular by the social Web. Users rank favorite
items by tagging them with freely chosen keywords, and as numerous users tag the same item, its categorization emerges).

This type of social networking is spreading from Gen Y to
all the other generations in the online environment, as noted
in the Introduction. The bottom line is that Web 2.0 is creating
new opportunities for innovation.

Venture capitalists and other financiers are looking to back companies with the following features in attractive industries: large and growing, products for which customers have a high need, younger industries, high operating margins, and markets that are not crowded. The Web 2.0 environment has attracted much attention, as it meets most of these criteria. The market is large, particularly if established companies are switching their focus to adapting Web 2.0 technologies. One challenge, however, is determining whether or not customers will have a need for the particular products or services offered by new Web 2.0 companies—specifically, can customers envision what they need if they don't ask for it first? In the traditional approach, businesses arose to solve existing problems for customers, but in the Web 2.0 world, companies are offering new and previously unimaginable possibilities to individuals instead of seeking to solve established needs.

To determine the level of customer interest in new ideas, entrepreneurs often conduct primary and secondary research. First, they should analyze industry participants and potential customers; then, they should look at similar situations for which data has already been collected. The difficulty of conducting research for "breakthrough products and services" is that the market does not exist, so, therefore, secondary research is unavailable.

A second issue to consider is market timeliness. Entrepreneurs need to look at who is in the market and whether or not a window of opportunity exists. For a breakthrough product or service, speed is important in order to gain the so-called first-mover advantage. Cambrian House, along with a number of the other Web 2.0 companies examined in this book, believes that the first significant company in the market can gain a sometimes insurmountable advantage. At the same time, there is also a "second-mover advantage," because the initial competitor can study the first mover's mistakes and subsequently introduce small-but-important improvements. The second-mover advantage is a justifiable concern for first movers in today's environment, because transparency is highly valued in the marketplace but it also increases competitors' access to valuable information.

A third issue to consider is identifying a niche (or vertical) market within a particular industry. Of course, Web 2.0 will spawn a number of opportunities, but the successful companies will be the ones that identify a suitable niche. A "niche market" is a place within a larger market segment that represents a narrow group of customers with similar interests. One entrepreneurship text notes, "Most successful entrepreneurial firms do not start by selling to broad markets. Instead, most start by identifying an emerging or underserved niche within a larger market."[9]

There are two types of markets. First, a *vertical market* focuses on similar businesses with specific and specialized needs. In the online environment, vertical sites are those focused on specific interests such as baseball, painting, or dating. By contrast, a *horizontal market* meets a specific need for a wide variety of industries. An example of a horizontal market site is Friendster (the site referred to in Step 2), which had an initial meteoric rise and then floundered. The lesson to be learned from Friendster's fall is this: Avoid competing with major players head-on, and don't try to be everything to everybody.

Another important component of assessing an opportunity is to conduct an organizational feasibility analysis. This analysis determines whether or not a proposed business has sufficient management expertise, organizational competence, and resources to successfully launch its business.[10] Does the team have the management prowess to succeed? Two of the most important factors are passion—demonstrated by the leading entrepreneur and/or the team's management—and the extent to which the team's management understands the market. Teams with extensive professional and social networks have an advantage. Mike Sikorsky of Cambrian House freely admitted that one of the challenges in the growth of his company was creating an organizational design that matched the nature of the organization. Even though Sikorsky is an experienced entrepreneur, this was not an easy task. His crowdsourcing company started by pursuing different opportunities presented by the community, called "branches." However, he later discovered that his clusters of staff members did not have sufficient synergy if they worked too independently to develop the projects. In response, he reorganized the structure to better facilitate collaboration. Of course, because crowdsourcing is in its infancy stages, the pioneering companies have to work through growth pains.

Competitor Analysis

Although a business itself may seem viable, serious concerns may arise with competitors in the overall industry. How does Web 2.0 fit into that picture? In terms of industry, it is a relatively new phenomenon, and crowdsourcing is gathering steam. Thus, analysis of the competitive environment is critical. In the Web 2.0 field, company founders often hear that there are no known competitors; however, competition may crawl out from the woodwork. Although the Web offers great opportunities and an enormous market, there is also scope for competitors (whether high- or low-profile) from all sides.

Competitors may be existing suppliers who embrace the Web or new Web-focused companies. There are generally three types of competitors:

1. direct
2. indirect
3. future

Each founder must carefully analyze the competitive land-scape. One aspect of the feasibility analysis relates to whether or not the product/service can be delivered. For a firm considering a new product, the main objective would be to deliver something that is not being provided in the marketplace.

Yet another challenge when entering a new and rapidly developing industry is to identify actual and potential competitors. There may be few competitors at present, but how quickly could firms allocate resources in order to compete with your new venture? Plus, as a worldwide medium, the Internet abounds with unlimited opportunities—and unlimited potential competitors. As mentioned previously, the Web 2.0 summit reveals the international appeal of the Internet and its role as a leveling force for business ventures all over the world. The key is to use these factors in your favor by utilizing the first-mover advantage—acting quickly and providing a great product. Then, as competitors arise, overcome the second-mover's advantage by continually fine-tuning and adjusting your company's offerings.

There are three different types of competitors in the market. Direct competitors offer similar or identical products, which means both companies continually seek to "win over" customers' loyalty (and this is difficult to do). Indirect competitors offer similar products or services, but with a different focus. Lastly, future competitors are those who may allocate resources to the sector. These competitors pose a deadly threat to start-ups, as they are often large, well-financed companies seeking to expand an established base of customers.

The Applicability of the Six Principles of Crowd Power

Now that the overall landscape of the product or service, the industry, and potential competitors have been assessed, the next step is to review the principles of crowd power as applied to the proposed venture. There are three options with respect to the use of the threads of crowd power: Crowd power can be a core strategy of formulation, a tool of implementation, or neither. There are common principles of a crowd-powered site: core crowd power components, crowd parameters, ranking and evaluation structure, social networking, reward system, and individual profiles.

First, to be at the forefront of the crowd-power field, a company must have tools that allow the user to easily communicate and interact with other users and the organization. A successful crowdpreneurial company needs to be a vehicle for idea generation, and the crowd must have a platform from which to provide input on a variety of issues. As Jeff Howe told me, "If you want to be the room where the conversation takes place, then serve good drinks."[11] The environment should enable collaboration to produce viable, measurable, and community-controlled change in the most simplistic format possible. One example is Fluevog Shoes (*www.fluevog.com*), which allows its customers to participate with the brand by permitting users to design "open-source footwear." Users collaborate and suggest designs for Fluevog to incorporate into its upcoming product lines. Another example is Cambrian House, which allows users to share business ideas and proposals with other members to gain the insight of the crowd. Ideas are pooled and ranked according to user input, with the winning ideas gaining the funding necessary to bring the ideas to market.

Second, crowd power must be conducted within clearly established parameters in order to be successful. One blogger has
summarized a few rules for tapping the wisdom of the crowds:
Crowds should operate within constraints; not everything can
be democratic; crowds must retain their individuality; and crowds
are better at vetting than creating content.[12] The key objective
is to eliminate contributions that are not worthwhile and will be
time-draining for a company to deal with. You want to tap into a
diversity of opinion and not the mediocrity of opinion. My Jeff
Howe interview provides further feedback on establishing parameters of involvement.

A third aspect of utilizing crowd power is the ranking and
evaluation structure sometimes referred to as a "reputation system." This ties into the notion of transparency in the online
environment. The purpose of the ranking and evaluation component of the site is not to serve as a method for expressing
negative feedback, but rather to provide an unbiased assessment tool. What do people really think of the service? There are
various ways to organize feedback. A "recognition-focused"
approach allows individuals to recognize a group or person; who
is widely respected by the community. An "acknowledgement-
based" system gives credit to users who are doing the most in a
particular category. Another component is to facilitate "improvement potential," which permits the company to improve its stand-
ing with customers by changing components within its
organization that have been identified by the crowd. This allows the company to proactively interact with users to improve
its services. Another element is "fraud preventing," a system
that places a higher weight on users who rate and evaluate
more often and have greater credibility within the system to
prevent potential "gaming." Finally, there is "experience–oriented"

ranking, which focuses on individual user experiences with the company's product or service. For example, *www.dotherightthing .com* allows users to rate companies based on social impact by contributing relevant news stories pertaining to the company. Organizations are then assigned a rating based on how socially conscious they are.

Fourth, a successful crowd-power site should have a social networking component. Social networking facilitates community-building online, active engagement by members, and so-called stickiness—meaning that people have a reason to keep revisiting the particular site. But it is important to note that social networking can be purposeless, an end in and of itself. Crowd power, on the other hand, requires individuals to direct responses toward a specific purpose. In order for crowd power to be effective, the company's site must engage an active crowd that maintains an interest in the concept or project proposed. How does social networking happen? Individuals create profiles and begin to develop an identity within the site. They are then able to communicate with other users via comments, messages, or group postings. These individuals can then post their own ratings of topics on the site's ranking system, and they can contribute ideas for adoption. Well-known examples include *www.facebook.com, www.linkedin.com* (a Website that allows business members to connect with other people in their field or search to find other individuals in the network), and *www.greedyorneedy.com.*

A fifth aspect of crowd power, which will become more significant in the future, is to establish some method of rewarding individuals who are involved in the crowd-power process. The chapter on business models provides greater detail on this topic, but basically, individuals must have sufficient motivation to allocate time and energy to a Website. To encourage consistent interaction with the site, a reward system identifying beneficial contributions by each member needs to be developed. The user may receive points that affect his or her status, translate into money or company discounts, or increase accessibility in other aspects of the site. Furthermore, the user may receive points for commenting, posting and adding friends, hosting reviews of products or services, inviting new users to join, and so on. An effective site should promote networking and provide a tangible resource that identifies those who contribute the most, providing incentives for all consistent site users. For example, as mentioned earlier, Cambrian House rewards users with "Cambros," virtual money that can be turned into actual currency and royalty points.

A sixth tip for the effective use of crowd power is to establish the company's site identity with credibility, professionalism, and ease of use. In addition to these overarching characteristics, a company should aim to communicate a brand that is innovative, progressive, dynamic, transparent, inspirational, and collaborative. A crowd power company should ideally be free of any bias—nonpartisan, independent, and without religious affiliations. The brand should appeal to users from different generations (Gen X, Gen Y, and Baby Boomers) and different cultures, providing an accessible format that is easy to understand and cultivates interaction with the site.

All of these factors should contribute to tapping the "right" crowds in the "right" manner. If done properly, crowd power can have many positive benefits; if not, then a lot of time can be wasted sorting through marginal input.

NowPublic and "Progressive Feasibility Analysis"

A future billion-dollar company is growing out of a funky, lime-green office in Vancouver, British Columbia. The company is called "NowPublic," and it runs a citizenship journalism site with the tagline "crowd-powered media." It has spawned the largest band of journalists in the world. However, Mike Tippett, the managing partner, explained to me that this is not a collection of "actual news guys." Instead, it is an online network of more than 120,000 "citizen journalists" in more than 140 countries.

So what is crowd-powered news? NowPublic defines news as "new information on current events." NowPublic operates its site on the premise that there are three different types of news:

1. Original, relevant information about a current event that you have actually witnessed.

2. New information you have collected, arranged and contextualized about a current event.

3. Commentary, advice, or analysis directly related to a current event.

The news received from citizen journalists can thus be treated accordingly.

The value of a company such as NowPublic is particularly demonstrated during situations of severe crisis. Tippett explains that during the Hurricane Katrina crisis, NowPublic had more citizen reporters in the area than many news organizations did. In fact, if the news organizations had sent all of their staff to report on the event, the number of staff members would still have paled in comparison to the number of citizen journalists on the scene. Tippett's international band of reporters records what is happening on location all around the world. Because of its success, NowPublic is currently expanding its partnership with the Associated Press (AP) to include AP's bureaus across the United States. AP is the world's largest newsgathering organization, with a staff of more than 4,000 employees located in more than 240 bureaus in 97 countries. NowPublic started an innovative partnership with them in March 2007.

Tippett cofounded the company with two other partners, Leonard Brody and Michael Myers, although he describes himself as "the guy in the garage"—and yes, it did actually start in a detached garage.[13] He used to live in New York City, and he remembers posting pictures of 9-11 survivors on the Website of his previous company as a way of connecting people.

Today, NowPublic is a great example of crowd power in action. Crowd power is a core strategy of the company and a tool in strategic implementation; in fact, without crowdsourcing, the company would not exist. The citizen journalism concept also ties in with the current trend of news generated by the people and for the people, such that people can see what is interesting to them instead of what an organization deems newsworthy.

How did Tippett come up with the idea, and what type of feasibility analysis did he do? NowPublic started with three partners, including Tippett. Tippett had been doing "Internet stuff" for about 13 years. He started to get interested in blogging and remote wireless devices. At the same time, wi-fi technology and camera phones were gaining popularity. He understood the technology, so he started blogging about it. He also noticed Websites for people who liked to post snapshots from their camera phones and make up headlines for the images. Combining the two elements together, Tippett set up a small portion on the back of his site that enabled people to post camera photos in conjunction with top news stories. He realized that this new aspect of his site was gaining unusual popularity. In fact, the feedback showed that site visitors didn't care what he had to say, but they were very interested in other people's postings about the news. Thus, the idea of NowPublic was basically a response to the interests of his "customers."

Tippett instinctively adopted a very customer-centric approach to determining if he had a worthwhile opportunity. He notes, "It is foolish to try to be too prescriptive or too strategic. I think successful Web 2.0 companies are more tactical." He explains that Flickr went through the same formulation process: "The Flickr site started off as a game, and part of the game was a shoe box that you could put your photographs in. The site founders realized after a while that people weren't that interested in the game—they were more interested in the shoe box. So Flickr came to the accidental realization that people were interested in sharing photographs."[14] Today, Flickr is a tool that lets users bookmark images they are interested in and generates an RSS feed from what users are reading.

According to Tippett, "The reason you set something up is not always the reason people will use it for. You have to be very receptive to the signs [of customer interest]: Even though you have a certain amount of traffic, you have to figure out exactly what people are looking at. In my situation they were looking at photographs and not my writing."[15] Despite all the pre-planning that goes into a venture, Tippett's example shows the importance of understanding your customer base and listening carefully to their priorities.

In effect, Tippett adopts a discovery-driven planning approach, referred to in Step 1. I prefer to use the term "progressive feasibility analysis." Tippett has continued to expand NowPublic in response to the input of the crowd; the feasibility of any corporate move is conducted progressively with the crowd. This is a parallel process. On the one hand, he has established broad overall business objectives for NowPublic by setting a goal for the number of people visiting the site by a specified time, aiming for a certain amount of revenue, and developing certain levels of profit margins. But on a different level, he believes the road to success must be discovered one step at a time, with an awareness of your customers acting as a compass for your progress.

Tippett states, "Part of the mystery of Web 2.0 is that many of the assumptions you have about human nature and the way people interact with their property and other people's property are counterintuitive." For example, he cites the idea of people devoting time and energy to sites without being paid: "The whole idea of the gift economy, sharing and giving away for free, is outside of the traditional business mindset. You have to be open-minded about it, because it can be scary as an entrepreneur; you may not know what you are getting into." His conclusion is that the real risks are not technological, because you can build anything you want; rather, the big risk is what happens when you put your idea into the market. Tippett describes the key issues: "Is the market going to be receptive to your idea? Because everyone has his own sense of what people want. People may be watching your site, but they may be watching it for a different reason."[16] So, for an entrepreneur considering a Web 2.0 opportunity, there should be sufficient research to launch the process, but no so much as to project with great detail how it will evolve.

In short, the notion of crowd-empowered behavior turns the conventional feasibility analysis on its head. Although entrepreneurs typically conduct an analysis at the outset—at which point the costs of a decision are weighed, resources are allocated, and the entrepreneur proceeds with the green light from investors—crowdsourcing does not function in the same manner. Crowdsourcing involves ongoing incremental action tied into the responses of potential customers. Thus, the initial feasibility analysis for a crowdsourcing start-up is primarily to determine if the overall framework of an idea is worthwhile, within which an incremental feasibility analysis can take place.

Step 3 Recap

✓ By adopting a crowd-oriented approach, an entrepreneur can eliminate considerable risk in the feasibility process.

✓ An entrepreneur needs to determine the feasibility of the product or service by analyzing the overall industry, the particular market segment, and the competitive landscape.

✓ With this conventional analysis as a framework, an entrepreneur can then examine to what extent the six principles of crowd power apply to a particular venture.

✓ NowPublic and Threadless are examples of companies that conducted a "progressive feasibility analysis," an option that is only practical in our new Web 2.0 world.

Feature

An Interview With Mike Tippett, NowPublic and
Crowd-Powered Journalism
(In Vancouver, BC, on August 24, 2007)

Please note: Abridged portions of this interview are used topically throughout this book. The unabridged interview is included to provide a contextual reference for the sourced passages.

Richard Goossen: Who are the partners of NowPublic?

Mike Tippett: Besides myself, there are two other cofounders. One is Michael Myers, our CTO, who lives in New York; I have known him for years. The other is Leonard Brody, a friend and very experienced and successful investor in high-tech companies.

RG: How did you come up with the idea?

MT: I think the idea came from my basic approach to the businesses that I get involved in. I am a firm believer in listening to your customers—even before you have the first customer! The history of NowPublic is that the three of us founded the company together. I am the guy who started in the garage; and, yes, it actually was a detached garage. I have been involved in Internet businesses for about 13 years. I lived in New York for a while and then I came back to Vancouver to see where the wind would take me. I started to get interested in blogging and remote wireless devices. At that time there was this explosion of wi-fi products and camera phones were becoming more popular. I felt that this was an area I could understand so I started blogging about it. My idea was just to blog about how these wireless devices would change our lifestyle. However, as part of that I noticed that there were all these camera phone sites where people would post their snapshots, and in many cases they would mash out headlines to go with the photos. So I set up a small portion on the back of the site that was camera photos mixed in with the news. When I looked at the blog files—and this ties back into the idea of listening to your customer—I realized that people didn't care that much about what I said on my blog. Instead, people were very interested in what other people had to say about what was happening within the news cycle.

RG: What was your strategic approach as to pursuing this idea?

MT: As I mentioned earlier, I took a customer-focused approach. I think it is inappropriate to try to be too prescriptive or too strategic; there is a limit to how far ahead you can do strategic planning. I think successful Web 2.0 companies are more tactical, responding and readjusting their approach based on constant reading of customers' requirements. Flickr is an example of a company that takes this approach. Flickr started off as a game. Part of the game was that they had this shoe box that you could put your photographs in. They realized after a while that people weren't that interested in the game as much as in the shoe box. So Flickr came to the accidental realization that people were interested in sharing photographs through a tool that let users bookmark something they were interested in. So people were using it for that purpose. Then Flickr also realized that this tool was a great way of generating RSS feed from what users were reading. My realization, and I applied it to the development of NowPublic, was that the reason you set something up is not always the reason people will use it. My conclusion was that you have to be very receptive to reading the signs of what is happening on your site. Even though a site might have a certain amount of traffic, you have to figure out exactly what people are looking at, and, in my situation, they were looking at photographs and not my writing.

RG: What is the implication of this approach for strategy (that is, to "see where the crowd will take me")?

MT: On the one level, I think a company can have broad overall business objectives. For example, you can set objectives such as the number of people to visit a site by a certain time, a certain amount of revenue, and to achieve certain types of profit margins. But, on a different level, I think the way you get there is often something you have to discover step by step. I think part of the mystery of Web 2.0 is that many of the assumptions you have about human nature and the way people interact with their property and other people's property is counterintuitive. The whole idea of the "gift economy," open source, sharing and giving away things for free, is outside of the traditional business mindset. You have to be open-minded about it, because as an entrepreneur because you may not know what you are getting into. The real risks are not technological because you can build anything you want. The big risk is what is going to happen when you launch into the market. Is the market going to be receptive to your idea? Of course, everyone has their own sense of what people want. The challenge as an entrepreneur is that you often find people are watching or using your site, but possibly for different reasons than you expected.

RG: Do people get compensation for the stories they post on NowPublic?

MT: As a matter of course they don't. There are exceptions, however. For example, we have a deal with the Associated Press, the largest news organization in the world, that if one of our members sends in a fantastic video or photograph that gets picked up, then AP will pay for it. This provides an opportunity for our members to make money, though it is by no means guaranteed.

One of the objectives of NowPublic is to start expanding the avenues through which people can make money, whether it is through lead stories or ads from pages they generate. Right now, however, the way of getting paid is through our partners who are in the business of paying for content. A separate way of generating money is that occasionally people will "tip" members for a story, just like you would tip a waiter.

RG: How important is compensation? Will there be a backlash?

MT: That question is difficult to answer. While people always appreciate some form of payment, Web 2.0 companies typically aggregate content from users without paying for it. Google, for example, is a leading aggregator of user-generated content, from university sites to individual and company sites—but they don't pay for it. Google is the largest media company in the world because they can make money through advertising. I think the key for NowPublic is to make sure that the people who give us content are given some sort of positive benefit.

RG: What motivates people to contribute?

MT: This is the hardest nut to crack. We have found that there are four major reasons that people contribute to sites. First, there is a small group of people who are providing submissions on a quasi-professional basis. These people want to get paid what they can for their contributions.

Second, there is another group of people who are not pro-viding submissions for the money, but they want some sort of stamp of approval of having been paid something for their work. This is a non-professional journalist who wants to get recogni-tion or credibility through our sites. People may only get paid a nominal amount for a story, such as $10, but it signifies that they have made a worthwhile contribution.

Third, there are a number of people who will realize that they can make a bit of money without too much expertise or effort. They can get involved in the process as a passive participant and get a couple of bucks per month. This is almost like an AdSense type of funding where you are making, say, $10 per month. This is something that is on our site now and that will grow.

Fourth, there's another group of people who will just do it for free and send it along.

Regardless of the specific reasons for contributing, an overall theme is that most people who contribute view the process as a means of self-expression. In some instances they want personal fame or recognition. In other cases it would be the same sense of motivation as when people are having a conversation, simply to have their opinion heard. It's just like exchanging ideas at any gathering of individuals, whether at a bar or a coffee shop. People are social and they want to connect with other people. In some instances, where tragedy has struck, people may be doing it for somewhat therapeutic reasons. For example, after Hurricane Katrina we had thousands of people posting stories. We have discovered that after catastrophic events, which are typically newsworthy, people will talk about it.

RG: Is there an anti-establishment aspect to contributions provided by your members?

MT: There are two types of content.

First, there is politically motivated content. A person may think that a particular story that is newsworthy is not being covered in the mainstream media. Some people feel that there is a political agenda attached to mainstream media in terms of what types of stories are allocated the most coverage. We have not positioned ourselves as feeding that agenda, however. We want to be politically agnostic. We want to be a platform for people rather than promoting a particular agenda. In that respect our approach is different from many blogs which are ideologically driven.

A second, and more interesting type of content is based on "the long tail" concept. There is a lot of content that would have been impossible to cover previously due to economic reasons. The crowdsourcing of news works because we can report on stories that were not economically viable before. In that sense we are antithetical to mainstream media; we can report on events that they simply cannot cover. This, however, is an economic reality rather than a political motivation. This is a big opportunity because there are many activities going on (that is, reunions, and so on) that simply cannot be covered by mainstream media and that people are passionate about and interested in.

RG: How long has NowPublic been crowdsourcing?

MT: We had the company for two and a half years already before the term "crowdsourcing" was coined. Crowdsourcing was a buzzword we were looking for; we just weren't smart enough to coin it. In many circles, crowdsourcing has become a household word, so it offers us a form of shorthand to explain what we are doing.

RG: Why use the term "crowd-powered" rather than "crowdsourced" news?

MT: We decided not to use "crowdsourced" news as we wanted to emphasize the notion of empowering people. We thought that "crowd-powered" was a positive notion. By contrast, crowdsourcing seems to be more of an economic term that is related to the ability of businesses to reduce costs, which is how the related term "outsourcing" is often perceived. Instead, we wanted to emphasize the fact that people are now empowered to participate in the process, rather than having them believe that work is simply being outsourced to them.

RG: How did the company grow so rapidly in a relatively short period of time?

MT: First, we got in quite early and we had a first-mover advantage. We were able to establish our NowPublic brand in the marketplace. At the same time, being first can be a disadvantage, as we were breaking new ground. The usability of our site was originally terrible and we had to fix a number of problems.

Second, we have a good company name. "NowPublic" leads people to perceive that we are trying to do something good. We have found that trying to be ethical and to make positive change in the world is a very powerful marketing ally. I think the positive perception of the company is critical to allowing us to attract and retain really good people, get lots of members, and I think it even helped us with respect to our financing.

Third, I think a lot of our success has been based on listening to people. For example, we would go to Flickr and YouTube and say, "you have a great photo or video on a news story," and we would ask if they were interested in sharing. They would say, "no problem" but then people couldn't find the photos or videos on their hard drive. So, by listening to our members, we resolved to build a tool that would remedy this.

Fourth, we have been integrating ourselves into the evolving Web 2.0 ecology and trying to understand customer behavior, best practices, and leaving behind our prejudged assumptions. We have realized that the right response for our company is not always obvious. As I explained earlier, you wouldn't think that a barrier to contribution would be that the person forgot where the picture is in their hard drive. You might think instead of how much to pay a person for their contribution or to protect their loss of rights over a picture. There were a number of instances where we went through a learning curve. We figured out what the obstacles were to people participating fully in the site and successfully addressed them.

RG: You need to respond quickly?

MT: Absolutely. The customer is really in control these days. The more you leverage that, the better off you will be; the more you resist that you are in trouble.

RG: How did you ramp up the site?

MT: First, the growth of site traffic has been fairly steady but there have been a couple of inflection points. When we first started we had considerable buzz. We were helped by what I call the "Gang of 100,000" in Silicon Valley. These are the people on Technocrati, the first people into Flickr, they are the people who go to the Web 2.0 conferences, and who really influence tastes in Silicon Valley. Buzz can be personality-driven and technologically driven. For example, David Winer, the guy who invented RSS, has a blog that is a bit obscure but highly influential. Winer has expertise and credibility on technological issues, and a lot of those people subscribe to Winer's RSS feed. Those influential people may have their own blogs, which may then become the most popular tags of the day for social bookmarking sites such as del.i.cious (*http://del.icio.us*).

We were helped by being part of that network in the early stages of the company.

Second, it was important that our network of connections thought that we had a really interesting idea. We wanted to get buy-in from the people who are the thought leaders and who are influential.

Third, Hurricane Katrina was an inflection point in the development of our site traffic. One result of my personal experience of living in New York when 9-11 happened was that I realized the need for communication and reporting during a time of crisis. When Hurricane Katrina was approaching, we said that if things go badly, we need to be prepared with the technology to do tagging and posting photos and provide a vehicle for missing persons. Despite our preparations, our servers were overwhelmed— yet we rebounded quickly. As a result of our extensive and timely news coverage of the event we provided information and were cited in 60 to 70 newspapers worldwide. Almost instantly our company profile was elevated. We could never have afforded to buy that type of publicity. From an economic perspective our coverage of the event was a huge win for us. At the same time, our motivations were not driven by business interests, but rather to help people. One lesson I learned is that sometimes doing the right thing can also be financially rewarding.

Fourth, our site benefited from publicity-generating opportunities that became available to the company as a result of our heightened profile. For example, some members of the academic community became interested in studying the company and in publishing their findings. I also began to have the opportunity to speak at various conferences.

RG: How will you continue to grow the company?

MT: We want to build the largest news organization in the world. Even right now, our number of citizen journalists would dwarf the news staff of any other news organization. Is this an "apples to apples" comparison? No. We have some highly qualified news people, but it is a mixed bag. If a subset of those people can establish some type of credibility, then it will be an "apples to apples" comparison.

We have two goals that will propel the future growth of NowPublic. First, we want to create a huge group of citizen journalists so that when news happens anywhere in the world we will have someone there. Second, we want to foster a subset of credible people who will get the stories right. We will then become a credible, well-respected news service, along with our global coverage.

RG: How reliable is your news coverage?

MT: I think we are comparable to Wikipedia, which has volunteer contributions as we do, and yet is basically as accurate as other available sources. I think challenges to the accuracy of our reporting system are the result of a rearguard action by entrenched interests who are attempting to preserve a notion of centrally controlled media.

Developing an Effective
Crowd-Power Business Model

Bruce Livingstone, founder of iStockphoto (*www.istockphoto*
.com), turned his passion for photography into a $50 million pay-
day within 6 years. IStockphoto is a Web 2.0 company that revo-
lutionized the stock photography industry worldwide. They
provided an innovative solution for the distribution of photos
from non-professional photographers to a global marketplace. In
the process, they helped photographers make money, and designers, nonprofits, and small business owners save a lot of money.
At the same time, many professional photographers were on the
run or out of business—what they were selling for $100 a person
could now buy for $1. Hard to compete with that.

Livingstone had a passion for photography. His site enabled
the distribution of royalty-free photos starting in 2000. At first
this was solely a passion and not a business. In February 2002,
Livingstone explained to the online community that he needed
to generate revenue to sustain the site. The community decided
to charge $0.25 per photo, mainly to cover site maintenance
fees, with 20 percent of charges going back to the photogra-
pher.[1] Only in 2004 did iStockphoto become a for-profit entity.
The business model has since changed; commissions vary from
20 to 40 percent depending upon sales volume and whether or
not iStockphoto has exclusive rights to the images.[2] Today, photos sell for $1 to $20, and they have approximately 2.7 million
photos available.[3]

IStockphoto exhibits one of the key hallmarks of a Web 2.0
company: It has created a vigorous online community focused
around a central passion, such that members are contributing
to the content of the site. The company was recently cited as
among the 500 most visited sites in the world, and was hailed as
"one of the first creative social networks of its kind."[4]

Although iStockphoto draws on elements of crowd power, and is often cited as a top "crowdsourcing" company, I do not view it as a crowdpreneurial company. Of course, it is a huge success—as a community of individuals using the platform. The critical distinction is that the members are not collaborating together for a particular project that is then part of the core strategy of the firm. IStockphoto would be a crowdpreneurial firm if its core business was tapping into its members to contribute pictures to massive collages that were then sold by iStockphoto as their business. Instead, iStockphoto is a platform enabling individuals to do business, from which iStockphoto receives a fee.

The story of iStockphoto at the start of this chapter demonstrates how a Web 2.0 business model was developed as the company evolved (the company started as a hobby site that later determined how money could be made). Getty Images, a purveyor of traditional high-cost stock photos, acquired iStockphoto for $50 million cash in 2006.

The Importance of a Business Model

The kernel of every business, and the key point of every investor presentation, is to address the basic question, "How do we make money?" I have read many business plans and witnessed many business presentations in which the answer to that question was not clear, not compelling, or not even addressed. In all instances, such a company is doomed. A company must have a clear conception of how it will make money. If it is a new venture and money-raising is key, then the projected way to make money must resonate with potential investors. In the vernacular, this is when the investor "gets it" or "the light bulb goes off in their head." The way to make money is a colloquial of speaking about the "business model" of a company.

A firm's business model is a combination of its competition strategy, proposed use of resources, relationship structure, and customer interface. The business model also addresses how a company will create sustainable value based on generating profit. A business model must be unique to each particular company and difficult to replicate. It is not simply some proprietary technology or secret sauce, but rather the ability to execute a plan of action better than other companies in order to serve a particular niche.

By nature of the previous description, a business model should be viewed as having a core, but it is not static. There can and should be ongoing improvements and modifications to a business model. After a proper feasibility analysis, the business model stage addresses how to surround the company with a core strategy, a partnership model, a customer interface, distinctive resources, and an approach to creating value that represents a viable business.[5] Successful performance is a function of both the type of business model and the execution intelligence deployed in its implementation.

A clearly articulated business model is important because it does four things.[6] First, it serves as an ongoing extension of the feasibility analysis (outlined in Step 3) by addressing how the company will create sustainable profit. *If this critical matter is not carefully thought out and substantiated, then there is no long-term future for the undertaking.* Often a conventional feasibility analysis will not unearth all the challenges to be addressed, so a business model will be recalibrated continuously. Second, a business model focuses attention on how all the elements of the business fit together and constitute a working whole. It keeps the company focused on its chief objective. Third, it provides a way to determine the key relationships for a company—all of which assist in making the business model work. Finally, the business model articulates a company's core logic to all stakeholders, from employees to strategic partners.

Components of an Effective Business Model

The dot-com meltdown resulted from the creation of many companies without a self-sustaining business model; they were relying simply on a hot market that seemed prepared to fund their money-burning projects in the moment. As then, and at the present, flaws in business models center around basic issues: Are there actually customers for the products? If so, how has that been determined? Is the business economically viable? How has that been determined? The steps outlined in this book are critical when it comes to developing and implementing a sound strategy for the pursuit of a Web 2.0 opportunity.[7]

The first component of an effective business model is for the company to clearly identify and articulate its core strategy. This is tied into the vision and mission of the company, as was discussed in the Introduction. After a company determines what it wishes to become and how it does its business, then logically it will be able to identify the core strategies required to fulfill its objectives. This process will provide a basis for defining the scope of the product or service of the company and its basis for differentiation in the marketplace. For example, the company can differentiate itself based on price, quality, convenience, and so on.

The second component relates to the strategic resources of a firm, one of which is the firm's core competencies—what unique aspects of the company's product or service help create a distinct market niche for the company? A firm must be able to do one or more things very well in order to maintain a competitive position. Another resource includes the strategic assets that are owned by the firm. Does the firm own a unique process, property, or other asset that is difficult to replicate? In short, a firm will try to combine both its core competencies and strategic assets to create a defensible competitive advantage.

Third, a vital component of a business model is strategic alliances and partnerships. This is a way for any firm, particularly a new venture with limited resources, to greatly expand its capabilities. Key strategic partnerships will allow a firm to have access to both personnel and resources of a specialized firm so that it will not have to devote its own capital to acquisitions. Some of these relationships may be on an exclusive or priority basis, which will provide further support for the firm's competitive advantage.

A final component of a firm's business model is the way in which it interacts with customers. A firm must carefully deliver value as it interacts with customers every step of the way, from telephone support to personal contact and follow-up. In some industries, customer interaction is one of the few points of differentiation for a company. In the airline industry, for example, planes for all major airlines are generally purchased from either Boeing or Airbus; thus, the most noticeable point of differentiation is not the planes themselves, but rather the interactions customers have with airline personnel.

Online Advertising and Marketing Strategies

The preceding discussion of the importance of a business model and the four components of the business model provides a general context for Step 4. Now we must look more closely at developing an effective crowd-powered business model. The first aspect to examine is potential online advertising revenue, which of course is available to any Website that draws traffic. Chris Breikss, a director and cofounder of 6S Marketing (*www .6smarketing.com*), has focused on online marketing and advertising strategies for the past 10 years; much of the information in this sub-section is based on my interview with him.[8]

Most Internet business models are heavily reliant on a successful advertising strategy, which is, in turn, tied to generating sufficient traffic to a site. Although there are other ways to make money online, I will focus on the advertising model. With the advertising model as a guide, the starting point for a successful online business is to generate as much traffic to its site as possible.

So how can a company obtain exposure for its site? A firm can try to establish itself with links on other Web pages—whether in the form of a text link or an image link that includes the firm's logo (these are called affiliated Websites, or "affiliates"). Analysts typically estimate that 1 percent of Website visitors will click through to a linked Website.[9] These links have another benefit in that they improve the link popularity of a firm's Website in search engines such as Google, Yahoo, and MSN. Essentially search engines such as Google, Yahoo, and MSN gauge a Website's popularity by measuring the number of links that point to the site.

As part of an agreement between a firm and its affiliates, the Affiliates should be required to include references and links to the firm's Website in their communication to their customer base. With a dedicated e-mail (an e-mail that is focused on link to the firm's Website), the industry standard ratios are that 12 percent of the membership will click through to the firm's Website and then become members/users of the site ("convert") at a rate of 10 percent.[10]

In some instances, depending upon the company, a supplemental direct mailing campaign may be beneficial. Many companies communicate with their membership via direct mail or phone. A firm may want to send out a promotional insert, and include the insert in its Affiliates' mail-outs, directing recipients to the firm's Website with a tracking URL that measures the campaign's success. According to conservative industry standards, approximately 1 percent of recipients will visit the firm's site.[11]

A site for a new venture should also have an aggressive search engine marketing strategy that will introduce first-time visitors to the firm's Website through a multitude of related key-word search terms. As well, a Website should incorporate dynamic optimization techniques to ensure that all user-generated content will instantly be made available to search engines such as Google, Yahoo, and MSN. This content should then be formatted into search-engine-friendly templates that are indexible to search engine spiders.

Overall, the search engine strategy is a long-term tactic that has the potential to deliver exponential traffic growth for years to come. A paid search engine strategy using pay-per-click (PPC) programs can also generate immediate interest and awareness in a firm's Website. In general, approximately 10 percent of visitors from search engines will convert into members of a new site.[12]

Related to the topic of search engine marketing strategies is the issue of selling online advertising. There are two options. First, a firm can use the Google AdSense program. Google AdSense is a tool for selling advertising slots to advertisers through the Google AdWords program. In essence, a firm uses Google to place ads on its site, and then derives revenue based on the number of individuals who click on those ads. This is like owning a billboard and letting someone else manage it, and you take a percentage of the revenue. Google AdSense is particularly attractive for new ventures due to the ease of its set-up and administration options. An AdSense account for a firm can be programmed to allow text, video, and image advertising in various sizes and formats. Custom channels allow advertisers to have additional control by providing the option to display ads in particular sections of the Website. Google AdSense advertising is configured as the "default" method of selling advertising; if the firm cannot sell advertising on its own, then the Google-placed ads will occupy the space. In this manner a firm can monetize every page view of the Website. This is an attractive option for a new firm, because it will not be subject to the commission that Google takes when providing advertising on the Google AdSense system.

A second approach is for a firm to manage its own advertising system. This is like owning the billboard and then selling and managing the space *yourself*. Here's how it works: The firm needs to develop an advertising management system to manage multiple forms of advertising. Advertising can be sold in multiple formats, including section sponsorship, cost per thousand ad impressions (CPM), or cost-per-click advertising (CPC). An advertising management system that allows the advertisers to log in to their own reports through an online interface and make creative edits "on the fly" is the most convenient option.

Some online companies also advertise by sending out e-mail newsletters to site members. An e-mail newsletter distribution system can also be used to manage the membership and ensure that a firm adheres to anti-spam legislation (that is, is not guilty of sending unwanted e-mail, and failing to provide a clear "unsubscribe" option). If a company chooses to set up an e-mail newsletter system, membership sign-up should include opt-in preferences that allow members to subscribe and unsubscribe from newsletters at any time. A firm must respect its database and strictly adhere to privacy policies.

Estimating traffic prior to the launch of any Website is difficult. A firm's traffic projections are based on a number of assumptions: the number of links from other sites; the interest from Affiliates to e-mail their membership regarding the firm's Website or to include the firm in their email communication; the projected success level of information in direct mail pieces with a drive to Web focus; and the projected success level of any online advertising campaigns with a search marketing focus. The primary goal of the Website is to convert any visitors into members by encouraging them to sign up for an account and provide their names and e-mail addresses. Of course, these numbers ("conversion" rates) are difficult to predict. Organic search marketing builds through time, with a limited amount of traffic estimated in the first six months. With user-generated content in search-engine-friendly templates, organic search engine traffic can become a major source of traffic toward the end of the first year after the launch of a Website. A successful stream of traffic is vital. After all, *if you can't attract a crowd, crowdsourcing will be impossible.*

As mentioned, the primary goal of a business-generating Website is to convert visitors into members. Website analytics tools such as Google Analytics and Google Website Optimizer can be used to strategize as to what is working and what is not. This will assist a firm in working toward optimal conversion rates from visitors to members. Along those lines, a firm's Website should offer incentives to encourage Website visitors to become members. Commonly this means certain elements of the site are available to "members only," while non-members can view a teaser that encourages them to join. Membership also frequently enables interaction with other members and contribution to the site in some way. That being said, a significant amount of content should still be available to non-members, but it should include messaging that motivates the non-members to sign up.

From there, the next step is to convert members into active members. Most visitors who become members have been motivated by an initial call to action. Once they have completed the task or item that was their motivation for joining, however, the Website will need to interact with them to ensure that they continue to engage with the site's material. In other words, the Website's features and functionality need to be interactive and "sticky" to keep members coming back for more. Inactive members may be prompted by system e-mails to encourage them to come back to the site. Also, members with incomplete profiles or members with stale profiles should be prompted to revisit the site. In the beginning, around 90 percent of members will need internal messaging, ongoing communication, and interaction in order to remain active members.[13]

As a site gains popularity (which it hopefully will), certain members may contribute more than others. Perhaps they interact with other members on a regular basis, post feedback, submit bug fixes, and use the site's features frequently. Many sites call these members "champions." As is discussed throughout this book, it is important to identify, engage and incentivize these members to help build the community. About 1% of all members become champions.[14]

The Four Elements of a Crowd-Power Business Model

The advertising strategies outlined here provide an important context for a crowd-powered business model. The advertising revenue stream is possible because of traffic generated by a site, whether or not it is crowd-related. This book gives examples of crowd-related sites that are able to generate considerable traffic.

How, then, does crowd power specifically fit into a company's business model apart from advertising-related revenue generation? There are four ways for a company to integrate crowd power into its business model in order maximize its income: Reduce risk by avoiding decision-making based on too little customer feedback; reduce expenses through participatory decision-making; enhance brand value and loyalty; and create additional revenue streams.

First, a crowd-powered business model can help companies reduce the risk of making uninformed, expensive decisions. A company with today's technology can ask the crowd for input on strategic decisions. For example, Fluevog Shoes proposes three or four lines of shoes each season and asks the crowd which lines are their favorites. Similarly, Cambrian House solicits ideas for new software products, narrows them down to a short list, and then polls the community as to which idea is best. This is, in effect, crowdsourced corporate strategy.

Second, crowd power can reduce in-house expenses by enabling companies to outsource to members in the crowd, who typically see non-monetary rewards such as status or creative exposure as incentives. Even when the company offers a monetary reward for the winner of a contest, running the contest is often cheaper than outsourcing the project. Thus, when a company secures the collective intelligence of the crowd, it can supplement its own resources. One example is InnoCentive, a crowdsourcing company launched by Eli Lilly (a large pharmaceutical firm) to reduce the costs of developing new medicines.

There are 120,000 members in the InnoCentive network, all of whom are required to register, give some description of themselves, and share their areas of interest. Members register as "solvers" in order to work on posted projects. Using crowdsourcing, InnoCentive can reduce its costs. It is unclear how long this situation may last as there appears to be a growing movement to provide some means of compensation to individuals who have contributed to the value of the enterprise. To date, financial compensation is generally symbolic, rather than providing a livelihood for contributors.

Third, the crowd-powered business model can foster brand loyalty. Typically, enhanced interaction and contribution by users enhances the loyalty of individuals to the product. The concept of directly including customers in the company community facilitates a sense of belonging among members. In Fluevog's case, members have demonstrated this sense of belonging by starting a personal network among themselves, not only with the company. The Fluevog brand unites and defines their community. InnoCentive fosters consumer loyalty to the company by encouraging site members (consumers) to make a personal creative investment in the company's future. While this is difficult to quantify in terms of a direct link between enhancing brand loyalty through on specific means (and a firm will have various methods) and the effect on sales, this is nevertheless clearly a positive feature for a company.

Fourth, crowd power can provide specific revenue-generating opportunities. There are not many models yet for ways to do this specifically. One of the few examples is Cambrian House, which is specifically focused on one thread of crowd power—crowdsourcing. Cambrian House expects to not only generate advertising revenue from its growing membership basis, but also fees from transactions occurring on its platform. The development of the Cambrian House model during a two-year period is follows.

Cambrian House and Two Years of Business-Model Development

Cambrian House is the best available case study for a crowd-powered business model, specifically with respect to the thread of crowdsourcing. The company has spent more than two years refining its business model and experimenting with new ideas. This is truly an example of business-model innovation, as there is no precedent to follow.

The business model of Cambrian House has a short-term element, related to immediate revenue streams that will add to cash flow, and longer-term elements, which contribute to the buildup of the enterprise value. With respect to the short-term element of the business model, in early 2007 Cambrian House explained its business model in three ways. First, "traffic is a proxy—we attract unique/targeted crowds." This typically consists of individuals who have "joined" the site by filling out a profile; their value is also reliant upon the amount of time they frequent the site. This ties in to the advertising revenue described in the previous section.[15]

Second, also in the 2007 presentation, Cambrian House mentioned that it intended to make money from its operating platform itself. In this capacity Cambrian House would be acting as an intermediary for people doing business on its Website. At the beginning of 2007, Cambrian House stated with respect to this potential revenue stream, "While the size of the market in terms of current revenues is small, the size of the potential market is forecast[ed] to be extremely large and commensurate with the amount of investment currently being applied."[16]

Third, the company noted that it also expects to make money as a participant in businesses that are originated via its platform. Founder Mike Sikorsky states, "Cambrian House makes money when we help spin something out. Part of that is an equity investment and the other part is participation [that is, the Gwabs video game described following]." Cambrian House is a clearing house for entrepreneurial ideas. He notes, however, "Since we are a small company with a limited amount of capital, there are a limited number of businesses that we can spin out— so we make money through the branches [division of the company described following]."

With respect to the last two aspects of the business model noted previously, the practice of sourcing ideas from the crowd and assessing which ones to invest in makes revenue projections very difficult. Although a crowdsourcing company will have proof of the support of it own "crowd," a company could not practically estimate the extent of the uptake of a product worldwide.

Another challenging aspect of a crowdsourcing business model is that as long as there is not sufficient money to cover monthly cash flow, then it is an experiment with a deadline. The company is well aware of this. For example, Cambrian House noted in a January 2007 investor document, though the details were not quite finalized, "After completing this round [$2.0 million raised by the end of April 2007], there is projected to be [approximately] 18 months of available operating runway."[17] Although a firm can work on developing the brand name, Website traffic, membership base, and an ongoing development of additional revenue streams, without ongoing revenue there is a limit to this pursuit.

Apart from the three short-term elements, there are two longer-term aspects of the business model. First, there is the buildup of the membership base of a company. Cambrian House materials highlight the value creation in the company through its membership base and high number of site visitors. Sikorsky explains, "We were loading up the value around the incubator for businesses into community members." With the present focus of the company, and based on comparables of community sites, he believes an accurate valuation of the company would be in the range of $20 to $40 a member.[18] This avenue, however, is only valuable upon the sale of the business; the hope is that a special purchaser will see the value in access to the accumulated membership base. A second long-term component is the value of the technology being constructed to facilitate crowdsourcing. An important issue in terms of the long-term value creation for the company is whether or not this technology is proprietary. Sikorsky comments, "You can't really copy the platform. It would be extremely painful to attempt. You could copy the basic ideas by looking at our site: profiles, badges, and so on can be duplicated. But the Chaordix operating system is our really deep, deep technology platform."

Earlier in the book we covered the four potential profit centers, or "branches," of Cambrian House. Now let's examine how each center operates from a business model standpoint.

Branch 1—Cambrian House Platform: the Chaordix Operating System

The Chaordix Operating System ("Chaordix") is the culmination of the company's ongoing refinement of its crowdsourcing platform as a framing structure that facilitates the generation, assessment, and launch of ideas and networking among its growing membership base. It intends to generate revenue in the following ways.

First, the company is proposing a fee based on transactions taking place on the site. Sikorsky remarked, "We are not sure what the percentages are, but we are going to let the community and market guide us." The idea of the transaction fee is as follows. If one community member has a company and another member offers to do a logo for $100, then Cambrian House will add a transaction fee of up to 1 percent, making the total cost around $101. Sikorsky doesn't want to discourage group postings by charging "listing fees," but he feels that such a minor transaction fee should not have a significant effect on members' business interactions. He estimates that in general that transaction fees would range from 0.1 percent to 1 percent of the value of goods or services exchanged.

The challenge, of course, is that adding a transaction fee means people must now pay for something they previously received for free. Sikorsky is confident that Cambrian House can make the transition. He recalls eBay's increased listing fees and notes that it ultimately didn't affect eBay's business, despite the fact that some power sellers revolted. According to Sikorsky, "If you're building something useful and compelling, you are basically going to have to charge for it. We have warned our community that there will be transaction fees."

Sikorsky also looks to the example of iTunes as his "saving grace." He believes iTunes has proven that, when offered an appealing mix of service and convenience for an appropriate cost, people who previously received something for free will indeed be willing to pay for it. Similarly, Radiohead's wildly successful "pay-as-you-please" download option for their most recent CD release, *In Rainbows*, shows that most people in the online environment have enough respect to pay for quality even when they're able to get it for free. Of course, there is also the example of iStockphoto referenced at the start of Step 4, which describes how the company evolved from a free to a paid service.

A second proposed component of revenue for Chaordix is distribution fees. Inside the Chaordix operating system, members can create a service plan and then use it to promote a particular product or service. When members begin to market their product or service, they place a value on it: for example, $10 a month or $100 to buy. Whatever amount the member is charging, Cambrian House receives 10 percent. In essence, this is similar to a conventional finder's fee.

Branch 2—Prezzle

Prezzle, the interactive gift box for "e-gift certificates," has tried a variety of methods for making a profit, some more successful than others. The original business model (which the company later would refer to as Prezzle 1.0) was to charge $0.97 per Prezzle-wrapped gift certificate and $5 to $8 per Prezzle when accompanied with physical flower delivery. Cambrian House was disappointed in May 2006 when a Mother's Day campaign that involved the selling of real flowers failed. The company also tried a New York foot-soldier experiment. As Cambrian House reported to investors, "We contracted a marketing firm in New York to hand out Prezzle flyers in hopes of creating an explosion out of the New York area that would virally spread westward, but the results only showed a minor increase in New York traffic. This has helped confirm our gut feelings towards a fully online marketing strategy."[19]

In July 2006, Cambrian House worked on Prezzle 2.0, which included a revamped Website complete with new Prezzle boxes and wrappings. The company reported that these met with minimal success, and in February 2007 the company reported that it was

reevaluating the current business model. At the company's Annual General Meeting in August 2007, Cambrian House announced that it would be working to divest itself of both Prezzle and Greedy or Needy (see following section). Both products remained under the blanket of Cambrian House with minimal administrative support. In late 2007, Cambrian House reported that the Prezzle site is now self-sustaining, and that the company is looking for a commercialization partner.[20] Prezzle's total revenue from inception in April 2006 until January 2008 was approximately $35,000.

Branch 3—Greedy or Needy

Greedy or Needy's original business plan specified that "In addition to 'wish' application revenue [individuals applying to "wish" for funds have to pay a fee], the Robinhood fund team is also attempting to secure revenue from advertising, sponsorship, and selling of qualified leads." The company implemented this method of generating revenue during the beta stage, but "chose to remove the $5 charge to make a wish" when the Website officially launched in January 2007. That, in conjunction with the site's revamped appearance, "resulted in over 1,300 new sign-ups in January alone."

Similar to the New York foot-soldier experiment for Prezzle, Cambrian House tried some in-person marketing to promote the Robinhood Fund. The company sent a team "to the streets of Toronto in January [2007] to help kick off the launch of the new site by delivering checks to the winners of the $20,000 giveaway." Unfortunately, the hand-delivery idea lacked sufficient payback on the cost and effort involved.

Cambrian House expected to generate revenue from online advertising and a direct donation charge of 10 percent when visitors gave money to the wishes. The challenge, however, was

to maintain the site's traffic volume. Priorities for the site were to continue "building community, enhancing user experience, and providing compelling human stories." As of July 2007, the Robinhood Fund had generated $1,452.68 in revenue over a one-year period. At that time the company decided to put a hold on direct donation charges.

At its AGM in August 2007, Cambrian House announced that (as with Prezzle) they would be working to divest itself of the Robinhood Fund. The Robinhood community continues to grow, and the company reports that Sony Pictures Television has commissioned producers to develop potential story lines based on its site.

Branch 4—Gwabs

Cambrian House expects to generate revenue from Gwabs through game sales as well as advertising via product placements within the game. In October 2006, Cambrian House established a Website to take pre-orders for the product. By October 2007, pre-orders for Gwabs totaled $1,011.06.

In short, Cambrian House has generated a modest amount of revenue throughout the past year—approximately $55,000, including pre-orders of products. The company has launched three branches—Prezzle, Greedy or Needy, and Gwabs—that have garnered positive feedback and are now poised for sale or further development. However, Cambrian House founder Mike Sikorsky believes that the chief source of revenue will be the Chaordix operating system. Its potential is great, but unknown. For 2008, Sikorsky believes that the company could generate advertising revenue and licensing fees of between $1 and $2 million. This would be a steep increase from 2007—yet in the context of Web 2.0, it is not unlikely.

Step 4 Recap

✓ Any venture that hopes to succeed in the new virtual market must have a compelling and practical business model.

✓ The four key components of a traditional business model are:

⇨ A clearly identified and articulated core strategy.

⇨ Strategic resources.

⇨ Strategic alliances and partnerships.

⇨ Customer interaction strategies.

✓ An online, crowd-powered business model. requires:

⇨ Online advertising and marketing strategies.

⇨ Improved strategic decision-making.

⇨ Reduction of expenses.

⇨ Fostering brand loyalty.

⇨ Revenue-generating opportunities.

Cambrian House is an example of an online, crowd-powered company with a unique business model that has undergone various stages of modification.

COMPANY PROFILE

Fluevog Shoes and the "Open Source Shoe"

"We receive over 10 million hits per month. We've obtained over 500 design suggestions for new shoes and hundreds of opinions on which lines of shoes to sell—over 2,000 contributions in total. And then there are the pictures. There are hundreds from all over the world where our shoes are being worn. Our online presence sells as much as one of our retail locations."[1] Stephen Bailey, marketing and communications director of John Fluevog Shoes, Ltd. (*www.fluevog.com*), recited those facts in a discussion of the company's online strategy.

Fluevog is a niche player in the global shoe market, and it has a cutting-edge business advantage. The company allows Website visitors to design their own shoes, with the incentive that any "chosen" shoe design will be marketed and produced—and named after its designer. "Fluevogers," as they are called, can also contribute feedback on shoe designs and company advertising. Moreover, these contributors have developed their own online culture, an international community of people united by the Fluevog brand and their passion for the company.

How has Fluevog succeeded in today's Web 2.0 online environment? By practicing the art of the crowdpreneur.

Introduction to Fluevog Shoes

John Fluevog founded his company 37 years ago in Vancouver, Canada, and has carved out an international niche for unique, pricy shoes. Though the road to success has been long and challenging, Fluevog has gained many devoted followers because of his eye-catching, quality product, and his savvy, ahead-of-the-curve marketing.

Fluevog explains that his customer base is statistically very small—especially in the U.S., where big-box retailers such as Target and Wal-Mart claim 80 percent of all clothing and foot-wear sales. He calculates, "That leaves 20 percent for compa-nies like us, and within that 20 percent, I'm guessing 5 percent of those are *possible* customers of mine—if I'm lucky. So, I'm not dealing with something that a lot of people want." But his com-pany survives by offering a distinctive and up-market product with a "signature" Fluevog look.

What is this unique look? As with many things, it's hard to describe, but you know it when you see it. Fluevog asserts:

> My biggest strength is that I've always had groovy stuff. The basic challenge is that I'm not selling a prod-uct that people need. I've always been a style-monger; I am selling a feeling and an emotion. I've always felt that I've known why people want to spend more money than they need to. From there it's a see-saw so as to not make my products so far out that the average person can't "get into" them. And yet I can't make them too ordinary, or I run into price competition. So I'm positioned in a very specific market niche.[2]

The company has grown by catering to this particular client base in major cities throughout the world. Fluevog now has nine retail locations from New York to Los Angeles.

In order to thrive in the global marketplace, Fluevog needs to continually innovate; in fact, this is part of his company's product identity. Furthermore, Fluevog's creative approach to shoe design needs to be equally reflected in the company's mar-keting and communication strategy in order to succeed in a highly competitive marketplace.

Fluevog has grasped the potential of the Internet for a number of years, because it is ideally suited for a niche player such as himself: A cost-effective online presence allows him to market to an international clientele. But using the Internet as a tool has evolved for Fluevog. Following the overall trend from Web 1.0 to 2.0, his company has shifted away from a static list of product information to feature an interactive vehicle that engages its devoted customer base and enhances customer loyalty. How has Fluevog done this?

Tools and Crowdsourcing

One aspect of the present Web 2.0 world is mass collaboration and its various derivatives. Companies are discovering the value of the crowd not only in terms of posting information, but also in the context of idea generation and collaboration of specific projects.

Fluevog has acted in a crowdpreneurial manner. Their site engages customers from the creation of the product, the launch of the product, the sharing of user experiences, and direct interactions with company personnel. The company's Website allows numerous opportunities for consumer input. Through sourcing the crowd—site visitors or members—Fluevog allows potential customers to contribute advice, creativity, and information to the company.

Fluevog's success as an online presence has not gone unnoticed: The site has been highlighted as one of the 10 leading crowdsourcing firms online.[3] Fluevog has successfully integrated crowd power, and specific elements of crowdsourcing, into the strategy of a conventional retail firm with "bricks and mortar" locations (as opposed to firms that use an online presence as the basis for their formation, such as Amazon did with books).

But what is Fluevog doing in a more specific way to practice the art of the crowdpreneur?

Fluevog has implemented crowd power as an online tool in three specific ways. First, there is a program called "VogPopuli— The Voice of the Fluevoger."[4] This, of course, is a play on the Latin term "vox populi," the voice of the people. Vog Populi is a forum where the company poses questions to the crowd. The Website explains: "Yes, Fluevogers, you are part of history. This is where Fluevogers from all over the galaxy convene to make their voices heard—and heard you will be. From time to time, we're going to seek your wisdom and counsel on a current decision, from ads to shoes, colors to cake mix. Nothing like a galaxy of Fluevogers to keep you in line."[5]

The questions posed thus far have included which shoes the company should produce and which magazines the company should advertise in. Amazingly, the company has received more than 2,000 responses within a week of asking a single question.

Second, a page called "FlueShots" allows Fluevogers to post pictures of themselves wearing certain shoes. The Website explains:

> Given the variety of Fluevogers out there, we wanted to give you a place to show your face (and your vogs) to celebrate your Fluevogian background. We know you've got some prime shots decorating your computer that are begging to be shared with the world in a place where they can be with other like-minded photos. Tell us your name and city and upload your shots. (Nothing vulgar please, as Fluevogers vary in age, hair color, and geography.)[6]

The photos have come in from all over the world, followed by comments from individuals sharing their travel experiences.

Third, and highest profile, is the "open source footwear" concept: Fluevogers can submit ideas for new shoes. This is the feature of the site that is closest to the nature of crowdsourcing. The Website explains the process:

> Is your imagination ahead of the whole shoe industry and you're sick of waiting for them to catch up? Here's your chance to go over their heads and deal with someone who actually cares what you want. All…you need is that brilliant idea. Even just for part of a shoe—scribble it down and send it to us. We don't care if it's on a bar napkin, as long as we can make it out. So, fax it, mail it, e-mail it, bring it in, just get it to us![7]

How did John Fluevog come up with the idea for open source footwear? Stephen Bailey recalls, "For years John would get ideas at the stores and trade shows on scraps of paper, napkins, and the backs of business cards."[8] He adds that devotees often wanted Fluevog to make a particular type of shoe. So going with an online crowdsourcing model was not doing something new, but having a more effective way of doing it. As the Web page states:

> And there you have it. Because we launched open source footwear, it's become one of the most visited pages on our entire Website. (The most visited is this picture of John, wearing only underpants.) We make selections through a combination of peer voting, feasibility, and if we just plain like the designs. Then, we cover all the costs and development process (it takes about a year to produce a shoe) and get your shoe onto the market, without having to put our prices up or go broke. Always a bonus. It's worked beautifully, and you've proven that Fluevogers have more to say than just, "Way rad, dude." You do it; we love it. Bring it on.[9]

The company has received more than 700 suggestions during the past 5 to 6 years, and they have accepted 12 or so, which they have made into actual shoes, available to the public.[10] Bailey mentions one lady who said that her car would make a great shoe! Her vehicle was a Volvo 240—and now Fluevog has produced the "240 Wagon" shoe.

Do the people who provide successful suggestions earn money? No. At first they simply received recognition; now they also receive a pair of shoes based on their design. Doesn't the company have to sort through a lot of chaff before getting to the wheat? Indeed, crowdsourcing must be carefully monitored and managed in order to be effective. Some ideas may be timewasters, but that is part of the creative winnowing process. At the same time, the company must maintain credibility: They must take customers' suggestions seriously. If the people have spoken and the company has not listened, then the well of ideas and customer interest will dry up. And once online credibility is lost, it is difficult to regain.

To keep ideas coming, the company must continually invent ways to increase the site's interactive capabilities. For example, Fluevog recently added a comment box on a contest entry form and received various comments from almost half of the entrants, ranging from bizarre to insightful. As online interest grows, the company must maintain that attention by enlarging its online community infrastructure.

Results and Crowd Power

What are the practical outcomes of Fluevog's crowd-power endeavors? First, crowd-power has facilitated online community-building. The language and tenor of the site create the feeling of a unique culture, one based on the customers' common enjoyment of Fluevog shoes. Members then develop a connection with the company—and even directly among themselves. Obviously, the focal point of this community is the brand and the product. Fluevog's online presence is now critical to its success; 48 percent of all Fluevogers visit the company's Website. In fact, the amount of revenue generated by the Fluevog's online business is equivalent to that of a retail location. But revenue is not the only consideration. Because of the community dynamic and the customers' own creative investment in the company, crowd-power also builds consumer brand loyalty. As people identify with the brand, they then become advocates for the product.

Bailey compares the Fluevogers' loyalty to that of Apple customers. Apple fanatics defend the product as superior to others, and die-hard Mac users build an identity for themselves based on the fact that they go against the flow—the mainstream 98 percent IBM clone users with the Microsoft operating system. Apple users find a degree of self-identification with the brand, and band together against non-Apple-users. In fact, those who identify strongly with a brand may also try to convert those around them. Bailey has seen people walk into a Fluevog retail location with a friend and try to sell shoes to that friend.[11] Such people feel a sense of shared ownership in the company—as creativity investors or "product" shareholders—and view a purchase as the invitation into a niche club of fellow customers.

This brand loyalty is enhanced through direct communications with the company. Bailey notes, "Simply being asked is important. People want to be heard, and we are listening."[12] The customers are now "we" with the company, rather than "them"; there is an interdependent friend relationship. Thus, by opening the doors to two-way customer-company communication, effective but crowd power builds deep customer loyalty. In addition, the company can identify its customer base in micro detail. Some may assume the demographic for Fluevog's funky shoes is limited to 18- to 35-year-olds, crowd-power responses reveal that Fluevogers range from teenagers to near-retirees in their 60s. Crowd power provides a window on their world; a direct way to figure out what they—the mysterious customers—are thinking.

Conclusion: The Art of Crowd Power

So, did crowd power create brand and customer loyalty? No. Did crowd power, however, provide a vehicle to facilitate community, brand loyalty, and increased sales? Absolutely. Fluevog uses crowd power in a careful and intelligent manner. The company is not built around crowdsourcing, but rather uses crowdsourcing to improve its current operations. In other words, the technology does not define the company, but compliments its objectives. Thus, crowd power is not the foundation of the Fluevog business model; instead, it is a tool for expanding the existing structure. John Fluevog has spent many years developing a loyal, niche group of customers, and the Internet now assists him by providing greater exposure and a means of meaningful collaboration with customers.

Step 5

Financing and
Growing the Company

If a crowd-powered company is generating minimal revenue and cannot cover its monthly expenses, but is building for the long term, will anyone, let alone sophisticated investors, provide financing? Yes. One such venture capital company is Rho Ventures, based in New York, New York and Palo Alto, California, which led a recent $10.6 million financing of NowPublic.

Rho has been backing emerging and high-growth companies since 1981; its venture capital and growth equity funds under management currently exceed $1.4 billion. Rho has invested in approximately 200 companies and helped build market leaders across growth industries. Rho was the lead group in a $10.6 million financing of NowPublic in July 2007. Why? "We're very excited about NowPublic's position to change the media landscape," said Jeff Grammer, partner at Rho Canada. "Across a spectrum of metrics—reporters, traffic, media distribution, and the like—they're executing beautifully on their goal of becoming the next-generation new network."[1]

Rho seeks to invest and participate in all stages of financing from seed to IPO. Rho selects investment opportunities based on the following characteristics: outstanding entrepreneurial teams capable of building extraordinary businesses, growing markets with revenue potential exceeding $500 million, market leadership with a high level of product/service differentiation, well-defined customer value proposition, high barriers to competitive entry, and scalable and well-defined business models.[2] Of course, a firm such as Rho has much to offer a company: a network of top-tier management teams, technology experts, advisors, and co-investors.[3]

NowPublic has minimal revenue, yet it is a pioneer in redefining the nature of journalism in the Web 2.0 world. But revenue is coming: NowPublic signed a deal with the Associated

Press with a payment per piece of content and also a general retainer agreement.[4] Mike Tippett's goal: "We think that this could be a billion-dollar company, and the way we get there is by building the largest news organization in the world." His strategy is "to focus on the bigger opportunity down the road, rather than some present options that might bring in some immediate cash." NowPublic has found experienced and patient investors, such as Rho Ventures, who are prepared to have the company "eat cash for the present, and allow it to keep building momentum and credibility in the marketplace, establish more alliances, an then become a large media company."

This type of transaction reflects the simple truth that investing in new ventures in emerging markets is conducted with a different set of parameters than buying, say, a manufacturing business with a 20-year history. This is the realm of entrepreneurial financing. Investors are those who see and invest in the future, rather than look at the immediate. As all seasoned entrepreneurs know, new ventures face many challenges in the process of attempting to get financing. Doing so in the new field of crowd-powered ventures and Web 2.0 technology may be even more difficult, as there are few successful precedents for reference. At the same time, there must be a sober balance. Most of the management team of today's venture capitalists and other financiers lived through the dot-com crash of 2000 and 2001. What lessons were learned from the past about investing in today's pioneering Web 2.0 crowd-powered companies?

Lessons From the Recent Past

The original Internet boom started in the mid-1990s and lasted until early 2001, when the precarious house of cards fell with a great crash. Previously, the delirium of the market had enabled Internet start-up companies with poorly conceived plans to attract funding—not because they had reached the bar for financing, but rather because the bar had been lowered. Dubious assumptions, which boosted financial projections, went unchallenged. After all, the Internet seemed to have limitless potential: it was a phenomenon never before witnessed, defying all the universal laws of business logic—until the universal laws of business logic smacked it right in the face. Charles Mackay and his descriptions of the "Mississippi Scheme" and "Tulipomania," referenced in the Introduction, would not have seemed out of place.

The bad aftertaste of the dot-com era still affects how investors view today's Internet deals. Although we have moved into the Web 2.0 world, entrepreneurs looking to finance their companies should heed the hard lessons of the recent past. In other words, companies looking for financing need to prepare plans that are finely attuned to the realities and realizations of today's market.

First, censor your business plan by removing any references to outmoded jargon. Beware the stench of rotting vocabulary; investors can smell it a mile away. The mention of simply getting "eyeballs" to a site is out of date; today the terms in use are "users" and "members." Although some crowd-powered companies may actually be in the "pre-revenue stage" they should have a clearly defined means of transitioning to revenue generation and building up the enterprise value fairly quickly. Similarly, investors don't want to hear that your "burn rate" is only a certain number of dollars a month. As noted earlier in the book, Cambrian House's Mike Sikorsky was careful not to use the term "incubator" when speaking to potential investors. A number of "incubator" companies received funding between 1995 and 2000, only to collapse in the dot-com bomb. While Sikorsky agrees that "a good company must be developed rather than instantly produced," he knows that "some investors consider [incubator] to be such a dirty word." Indeed, the company performs a similar function to that of an incubator, although it has a unique approach because of its use of crowdsourcing. Sikorsky likes to "phrase it like *Seinfeld*, which was a sitcom about nothing—and yet is one of the top sitcoms of all times." He remarks, "While our company seems to be about "nothing" right now, an investor can look at our talent and the process we use to find deals."[5]

The second lesson you can learn from the dot-com bomb is to be mindful of market timing. An entrepreneur should not come out of the gate too soon. Investors previously financed half-baked and ill-conceived plans just because the money was there. These "incubators" and "accelerators" were kites with no self-generated power, buoyed only by strong winds. When the wind stopped, the kites crashed to the ground. Now most investors think twice before throwing money at Web start-ups. An entrepreneur should not appear before investors unless the initial business model is well constructed, even taking into account the changes that will occur due to the "progressive feasibility analysis" discussed in Step 3. An entrepreneur should operate on the simple assumption that: The best way to convince a financier of the merits of your company is to show that your targeted client base is buying the product—today, not at some point in the future. This is the Threadless model; show that it is working on a small scale and that it can be ramped up. The key point for entrepreneurs is not whether they can attract financial support, but whether they can execute on the business plan. If an entrepreneur manages to raise funds but cannot achieve results, the financiers will not blame themselves for being over-eager. Instead, the entrepreneur will be stigmatized for future deals.

Third, carefully define your competitive advantage. "Legend-in-the-making" tales are a dime a dozen. Even though "Bob and his kid brother developed some world-changing software during recess and Bob's an expert because he spends his whole life playing computer games," there's a long and treacherous road ahead. More than likely there are many competing solutions for the same problem. Companies may claim they are unique in solving a problem, but that may not be the case in consumers' minds. For example, setting up "communities" on the Web was previously the rage. Many companies had grand visions for building worldwide communities with software that they believed to be "more complex and more scalable" than other offerings. Yes, and so was everyone else's. Then the talk was, "we're ahead by six months or eight months, and that's our competitive advantage." In today's market, however, a company's unique technology will be challenged very critically from both a technical and business standpoint. Having an interesting technology that can do "neat" things and impress technologically unsophisticated investors will no longer work.

A fourth point is to build a company—and not an idea. As it stands today, the Internet was largely a means to an end rather than the end itself. Internet companies with a real business can successfully use the Internet to further their aims, but their business is not "the Internet." Keep in mind that, online grocery delivery services have largely failed. Why? They started with the Internet and then worked backwards to develop distribution. In the meantime, the existing grocery stores had spent decades building distribution networks. Tough to compete with that. Actually, Amazon.com is one of the few examples of a successful company built on the concept of using the Internet as a distribution vehicle. In short, have a company and not merely an idea. You need an effective infrastructure for the successful commercialization of your product.

Fifth, present your technology or unique market niche in a clear fashion: What does it do? Who will pay for it? Why? In the dot-com era, many presentations featured the CEO's demonstration of his technology—after which the observers were perhaps not so much impressed as confused. The high-tech venture would claim, "This great innovation took six months of two software developers' time, whereas another company spent $5 million and couldn't accomplish the same thing." Today, on the other hand, the emphasis is on products that have already been successfully commercialized—investors have experienced enough bedazzling high-tech wizardry. Focus on the practical application of your product and the cost-benefit to the end consumer. You may have created a handy-cam with a host of fancy buttons and 10 different options, but most of your customers just want to point the lens at their subject and hit "record."

Sixth, have a clearly articulated business model. Address the issue as to whether the company will be generating revenue on a monthly basis, and what is the breakeven point. If not, then what is the payoff? If the value creation is in building a membership base and network, then map out how long that might take. Be realistic in terms of advertising revenue that can be generated. Many Web 2.0 start-ups are learning that site traffic does not necessarily equal profit. Ask yourself: Of all the Websites you view and use regularly, how would your habits change if you were charged for what you are now getting for free? Your answer tells you how much value you see in those sites, and how much potential those ideas have to generate revenue from viewers and users. As the opening example of NowPublic has shown, companies do not have to be making money in order to get financed, but they must show a clear path toward value creation. In the dot-com bomb, there was less of a base of knowledge and thus more reliance on the hype of the market. Today, investors are more savvy and experienced than in the last cycle—they still want to invest in the upside of getting in on the ground floor, but a company needs to show a clearer path to value creation.

Why, then, is Web 2.0 different from the dot-com bust of 2001? The Internet is no longer a novelty, but a ubiquitous reality. Investors realize, through the example of companies like Amazon, that business models may take time for traction, but that firms can be built with an Internet-based business model. There are many sectors for investors where patience is necessary to achieve a significant return. Investors realize that companies with a great strategy and an experienced team have the potential to do very well. The previous era did see a number of successes, but the excess of noticeable failures obscured the view of the companies that did succeed.

Sources of Financing

New ventures are often jumpstarted by utilizing the entrepreneur's personal resources and calling on the resources of the entrepreneur's family and friends. There are also various bootstrapping techniques such as leasing, accepting services in kind, and the like. Typically financing is necessary because the entrepreneur's vision is greater than his or her wallet. Thus, most entrepreneurs need others to buy into their vision in order for that vision to become a reality. Invested funds may cover initial cash-flow expenses (before the venture is able to generate sales), business capital, and/or lengthy product development cycles. In order to raise debt or equity, the entrepreneur needs to determine exactly how much is needed, whether to get it in debt or equity, and how to approach and appeal to the appropriate sources of that financing.

A new venture may receive funding from a variety of avenues. As an entrepreneur, you should be flexible and consider all sources of capital—and then determine which sources match the current state of your company's development. Keep in mind that potential funding sources will focus on their predetermined risk criteria. The availability of the options outlined in the next paragraphs will depend upon the state of your company's development.

First, perhaps the most obvious starting point is to *approach larger financial institutions*, such as banks. This may, however, be a fruitless and frustrating process. These financial institutions are interested in lending money to clients based on proper security, whether assets or personal guarantees. There may be some flexibility based on your track record. A clearly devised business plan and strategy will be helpful, but, as all entrepreneurs know, these financial institutions are not interested in taking risks and having losses in their loan portfolio. Commercial loans officers have clearly defined guidelines from which they waver at their personal peril. Avoid unnecessary frustration: Don't go to a bank with false expectations. Don't expect them to care enough about the potential of the business to override policies; they won't. They are not risk-takers, nor are they entrepreneurial comrades-in-arms—they are lenders of money and assessors of security.

A second source of financing is *sub-debt lenders*; these are specialized financial institutions that range from small boutique outfits to offshoots of household names. Sub-debt lenders typically provide unsecured term financing based on the cash-flow of the company and a personal guarantee of the founder. Unlike banks, they are not focused on hard assets of the company. Sub-debt lenders will often finance growth-related costs such as marketing expenses, management buyouts, on-going R & D, new offices, staff ramp-up, and inventory needs. This allows the company to conserve working capital without equity dilution. Some sub-debt lenders will provide financing simply as a term loan of up to five years. Other sub-debt lenders may provide a shorter-term loan, say of one year, with the purpose of seeing the company through to a public listing. In that scenario, the sub-debt lender may have the debt convertible to shares at a predetermined price upon listing. The sub-debt lender's rates are in the range of 15 percent per annum; their niche is to be higher than the bank's costs but lower than the cost of bringing equity into the company and giving up some degree of ownership.

Third, *angel investors*, who are generally wealthy individuals interested in privately investing in new ventures, may be a source of funding. Angels typically have experience with new ventures and have made sufficient money on their own to look at reinvesting. Most of these investors must be sourced through private networks, although more publicly oriented "angel investor conferences" occur in most major cities. At these conferences, founders present a series of companies to a carefully culled list of private investors. If an entrepreneur pursues this approach, then he or she needs to create a presentation carefully and in strict compliance with security guidelines. Investment opportunities cannot be offered to members of the "public" as it is defined within each particular jurisdiction. The most common exemption is for companies to rely on financing from private sources, namely "friends, business associates, and relatives of the senior officers and directors of the company."

A fourth source of funding is from venture capitalists (VCs), who are a magnet for people with growth plans. As noted in the introductory story regarding NowPublic, VCs such as Rho Venture will invest in new ventures. However, the criteria of VCs are a high bar to clear, as reflected in Rho Venture's specifications. VCs can receive 1,000 business plans or more per year, and they typically finance only 1 to 2 percent of them—so the odds are not in an entrepreneur's favor. VCs make their investment decisions carefully because they are entering into a long-term relationship with the companies they select. This relationship often spans three to seven years of financing. Because the VCs are putting down their money, they will not be shy about exerting control over the direction of the company in order to safeguard their investment. VCs often look at deals by size, geographical location, industry, and stage of development. Some VCs located in Silicon Valley will only invest in a company that is less than a two-hour drive from their offices. By industry, some VCs consider only e-commerce/Internet or wireless start-ups, while others prefer life sciences. An entrepreneur can position himself or herself to get into the top 1 percent, but it takes a lot of strategizing and putting the best foot forward.

Financing a Crowd-Powered Company

Although there are examples of crowd-powered companies that have received VC support, such as NowPublic, I will focus on the experience of Cambrian House to illustrate the financing process. I believe that NowPublic is an easier concept to understand—it is a crowd-powered form of journalism. People contribute online to the stories and they collectively provide their perspectives on the news. Crowd power is the way to make it happen. With Cambrian House, on the other hand, the focus is crowd power not only as the means but also the end. As a result, an investment in Cambrian House is truly an investment in the belief that crowd power has value and is the way of the future. Thus, Cambrian House is a more challenging investment proposition. But it has succeeded in telling the story.

How has Cambrian House raised approximately $8 million during the past two years? In order to raise his Round 1 financing (see the table on page 177), Sikorsky needed to explain to prospective investors that Cambrian House would spend a certain amount of cash before reaching the breakeven point, and that the value being created was on a long-term basis through the buildup of the membership base. He had to be careful with respect to his use of language, as noted in the previous section.

One of Sikorsky's advantages is that he has been involved in a number of start-ups as a principal, and he is also an angel investor in about 10 or so others. The message he delivered to the initial investors was a reflection of what he, as an angel investor, would have liked to hear. He uses a Calgary oil patch analogy: "Our approach resembled that of a great geologist who knows how to find oil.... I knew we could succeed if we let community members help guide development and market forecasting through crowdsourcing." His view of the company: "While we have some similarities to an incubator, we are more like an idea architect—we are guided by the hand of the marketplace and the hand of the community."[6]

Despite the great prospects for long-term value creation, investors like to see some specific markers along the way and often desire the option to exit so they have potential liquidity. As the initial investors have been invested for more than two years, Sikorsky realizes that the time for payback is on the horizon—not in the sense that investors would expect full payback, but in the sense that investors want some type of return. However, due to the fact that Cambrian House is a trailblazer in the field of crowdsourcing, Sikorsky candidly admits, "We don't know exactly how this is going to work."[7] His goal is *not* simply to be an interesting small company that incubates technology for a while before a large player snaps it up.

FINANCING ROUNDS

Round	Date	Amount	Price/Share
1	Nov' 05–Jan' 06	$2.63 million	$0.25
2	Dec' 06–Apr' 07	$5.3 million	$0.53
TOTAL		$7.93 million	

SHARE STRUCTURE

Description	Amount
Founders	$5,851,921
Round 1	$10,520,000
Round 2	$5,300,000
Subtotal	$21,671,921
Warrants	$1,886,792
Options	$ 3,250,788
Total	$26,809,501

SOURCE: Cambrian House Investor Presentation, Vancouver, BC (Spring 2007).

Overall, the situation at Cambrian House is a classic new venture story: huge potential but minimal revenue. As a result, the company has a "burn rate"—investors' funds get eaten up by the initial costs of running the business, and the time for recouping investors' money and breaking even looms in the distance. How does a new venture raise money under these circumstances? According to Sikorsky, investors need to know that it takes seven years to make a pearl. He explains, "I don't think there is any way around that. I'm not saying we can't have an early win." He cites examples such as Facebook and Google, both of which took a few years to get traction. The key, as these success stories have demonstrated, is to get appropriate investors.

In Sikorsky's view, "our investors have always been patient." Patient investors allow a company to build for the future and think long-term. Sikorsky comments, "The mistake we've probably made is that we always have to be thinking about our exit; this strategy would then be focused on building up the membership base as a foundation for an immediate sale. We actually think we can run this company for a long while, probably 10, 15, 20 years; this means that we are focused on generating revenue on a monthly basis in order to sustain operations." Sikorsky explains "the exit issue" with an elevator diagram. As the company rises toward the penthouse level (becoming an established leading crowdsourcing company), it stops at various floors so investors can get off early if they need to. The company will not try to make it from the basement to the penthouse all at once. Sikorsky says he and his team "think about these things"; moreover, "investors know that tech cycles can tap out sometimes at the top of the decade, like what happened in 2000." In simple terms, "When you are growing a company, you want to get it solidly to the next floor so you can unlock value if you have to."[8]

Sikorsky also believes he has the right investors on board. "I think most of our investors understood what they were getting into. If any want to get out, we are considering a share buyback auction. They may only make 2 or 3 times their money, but the ones who stick around get the 10 or 20 times return."[9] The bottom line a company needs to bear in mind is that a priority for any investor coming in will be knowing how to get out.

I asked Sikorsky if Cambrian House's company transparency policy, which is critical for community building, has posed a problem for investors. He responded, "If investors have a problem with our transparency policy, then we don't let them invest in our company! Even though some of our investors don't understand what our specialists are doing, they nevertheless encourage us to keep going, because what we're doing works." Sikorsky's goal is to continually create value in the company. He explains, "We try to create a positive, productive environment among our members by balancing rational exuberance with cautious optimism. That way there is always a good voice of reason. For those who don't understand why Web 2.0 makes money, they have just missed out on an exciting wave of possibilities."[10]

To sum up, a crowd-powered company, with minimal revenue and big potential, can successfully raise money. The company needs to find investors who understand the risk-reward situation and who are willing to be patient. As with any new venture, there will be challenges along the way. Part of navigating these challenges is to use a well-devised strategy for handling the constantly changing nature of the new virtual marketplace.

Strategic Planning for a Crowd-Powered Company

A successful financing plan must be matched by a great strategy. This is a component of "execution intelligence"—the ability to competently complete the steps necessary to reach objectives.

Ultimately, the favorable response of investors will be an endorsement of the strategic plan of the company. Cambrian House, in the spirit of transparency, has admitted some of its mistakes, but it has executed extremely well on its overall game plan. A key point for a crowd-powered company is that it must adopt the discovery-driven strategic planning approach discussed in Step 1.

First, a core strategy of Cambrian House was to establish the interest and allegiance of the crowd. The company explained to its first seed investors that, "Attracting a large number of community members has become an important strategic objective in increasing the valuation of Cambrian House."[11] In July 2006 Cambrian House launched with a great start: 4,135 community members, 1,909 ideas submitted, 195,904 site visits, and 649,900 page views. The company also engineered a publicity coup with its "Google Pizza video," which was the taping of the unscheduled delivery of 1,000 pizzas to Google's headquarters. The video received honor on YouTube.com and was listed as #37 in the "Most Linked (This Month) in Comedy." In short, Cambrian House succeeded in getting off to a great start in terms of traffic to its site.

Second, the company wanted to generate a wide range of ideas on its Website through participation of the crowd. The ideas were coming (approximately 6,600 as of February 2008), but the process of selection need to be improved. In September 2006, the company refined the method of selecting worthy ideas from the crowd. It launched "IdeaWarz 3.0," a monthly tournament enabling the community to better filter through incoming ideas. The concept behind the tournament is that voters select 16 ideas to battle. Less popular ideas gradually drop out, and the winner is eventually chosen. The company demonstrated it was willing to tinker with the workings of its site.

Third, Cambrian House was constantly looking for ways to develop revenue streams. In September 2006, Cambrian House established a "Virtual presence in SecondLife." SecondLife is a 3D digital online world imagined, created, and owned by its residents. Within Second Life, residents can buy and sell Linden dollars and own virtual land. Cambrian House joined to create another avenue for attracting community members. Sikorsky describes, "[We were] looking at it as a way to entice our community members to sign up for a paid subscription to the Cambrian House community. Currently, on average, more than $400 is transacted within a 24-hour period in SecondLife." In October 2006, Cambrian House created BattleAxe Island in Second Life. Although the income was minimal, the company kept searching for additional revenue streams.

A fourth strategic development was the decision, in January 2007, to change its approach to crowdsourcing. This was a significant decision, as it related to the soul of the company. Sikorsky acknowledged, "We were the bottleneck for many of our community members looking to start crowdsourcing."[12] They decided to get out of the way and let members do more commerce among themselves. The Website reads, "So—in a natural evolution, we're getting out of the crowd's way and building the community and tools to let them own their own projects, network with each other, define tasks, assign royalty points and more."[13] As a result, the company decided not to create internal teams to market tests and manage new products. Instead, the community will take the lead.

This decision has human resources implications. At the beginning of March 2007, the company had 34 staff working on its four branches: Cambrian House operating system (later Chaordix), Gwabs, Robinhood fund, and Prezzle. By the end of March, however, the company had laid off eight staff members for a total of 26. The objective of the staff reduction was to have Cambrian House operate as one tight team instead of as multiple teams that would manage the crowdsourcing of members' ideas. The company stated, "We found that with so many team members, managing communication and ensuring solidarity was difficult. We made the tough decision to let eight staff members go."[14]

The company repositioned its role from a participant in deals to that of an intermediary; consequently, the Website platform needed to be rethought. This was the impetus for the initial concepts of the Chaordix operating system, which began to take shape in April 2007. Cambrian House set the following goal as its brainstorming focus at that time: "deep thinking about how to create a 'sticky' and sustainable community, the decision to build a new, clean look, and a long feature list to add more value to members and create a product that we can use as a platform for upcoming member recruiting initiatives."[15] Again, this is an ongoing concern of a company. In June 2007 Cambrian House did further work to improve the site's user interface with the goal of attracting more members and competing with numerous emerging social networking sites. Cambrian House outlined that by the first quarter of 2008 it wanted to strengthen the focus on Cambrian House as the core product. The vision is as follows: "[to create a] platform that allows individuals and firms to harness wisdom and participation of crowds for commerce."[16] The milestones were outlined as building the operating systems kernel, solidifying beta networks, closing private beta, creating application partnership, generating increased revenue, and growing its membership to 100,000 members. The development of the Chaordix Operating System reflected the company's willingness to continually rethink every aspect of its model in response to the continually changing competitive environment.

Sixth, Cambrian House shifted its focus of operation from short- to long-term by becoming oriented to market entrance strategies rather than simply considering exit strategies. This strategy is a complement of the development of the Chaordix operating system; rather than trying to reward investors in the short term with sizzle and a quick sale, they became determined to build a more complex platform that would provide greater— but longer-term—value. As a start-up, Cambrian House was reliant on investor support. Often the first question of an investor is, "How soon can I get my money out?" (in other words exit). In view of the minimal prospects of monthly revenue, the emphasis for a new venture is thus on building up the enterprise value and then selling and showing a return to investors by way of a quick exit. The company decided, rather than focus on an exit plan, they would focus on building up the enterprise—this meant focusing on the core of the business, the Chaordix operating system. As a result, the company decided to divest itself of the Robinhood Fund and Prezzle. Further, they wanted to bring in partners to take Gwabs to market. The focus would then become to build and release the CH 3.0 platform with the goal of creating a vibrant ecosystem for commerce, crowdsourcing, and innovation with world-class beta partners.

The strategic-planning decisions of Cambrian House illustrate how a crowd-powered company needs to function in the new virtual marketplace. This is an ever-changing environment and there is no room for a static strategy. Instead, a crowd-powered company must be ultra-sensitive to Web 2.0 trends and the rise of competitors or changing circumstances. While a crowd-powered company needs sound strategic planning, it also needs to be mindful of the essential elements for company growth.

Eight Essentials for Company Growth

All skydivers are familiar with the term "death spiral." A death spiral occurs when a skydiver opens the parachute strap but it does not unfurl. The skydiver then begins spiraling downward in tighter and tighter circles, a whirlwind from which there is no escape. The same unrecoverable spin can also happen to entrepreneurs. I call it the "entrepreneurial death spiral." There are many pitfalls along the way of starting a new venture, and there are likely even more potential obstacles for a crowd-powered company. In response, I have compiled eight essential tips for a crowdpreneur to grow a company without falling into an unrecoverable downward spiral.

1. Accept Good Advice

Entrepreneurs may have been weaned on the notion that they truly know best—and sometimes their past success stories affirm their ability to prove naysayers wrong. However, as a general rule, entrepreneurs should seriously consider the insights of others. Without peer advisors, who will confront bad decisions? No one. Entrepreneurs make rules and hire their employees to abide by them, but outsiders can offer valuable advice to the entrepreneur. For example, banks can often offer sound advice to entrepreneurs as a counterweight to their unbridled enthusiasm. The banks' frame of reference is that they wish to preserve capital and earn a return. Banks are not interested in risk. They lend money. They want security. They want interest. And they want to be repaid.

2. Engage in Worthwhile Introspection

Entrepreneurs need to objectively analyze their individual and company performance from an external vantage point. They

184

must also be able to discern which sources of advice offer wisdom and which do not. In addition, a balanced set of opinions is critical for keeping ventures on track. If entrepreneurs surround themselves with supporters and push away dissenting voices, necessary changes will fall through the cracks—and the negative momentum will spiral out of control. Make sure you have a group of trustworthy advisors who can warn you of industry changes, rising competition, or consequences resulting from your own shortcomings.

3. Manage Your Ego

Don't let your ego run your company. Remember, everyone loves you on the way up—especially when they can make money from you. But on the way down, don't expect a lot of flattery. Have a balanced view of yourself that keeps both extremes in mind. When high-tech companies were pursuing their IPOs in the late 1990s, the press lionized the high-tech company founders. The founders' oversized egos led them to believe that they had truly attained unsinkable success. They failed to prepare for the storms—and when the storm came, they sank. It could happen to you, so don't delude yourself.

4. Remember the Core

What is the core skill that accounts for the success of the company? And what are the peripheral skills? For example, your company's core skill may be that you have talented people who know how to install a type of software for a better price than most others in the marketplace. Your core skill is not the fact that you have a group hug every Friday afternoon or gourmet pizza on Tuesdays. These fun events may contribute to employee morale, but they aren't your company's focus. Keep your eyes on the core and build up the expertise your clients want. After all, you can't support a corporate culture if your company isn't making money.

5. Resist Greed

Gordon Gekko, the icon from the 1980s movie *Wall Street*, proclaimed, "Greed is Good." In Hong Kong, greed is called the "red eye disease," and it has killed more deals than any other factor I can think of. Like the monkey who gets his hand permanently stuck in the cookie jar because he refuses to let go of an overstuffed fist of cookies—and thus forfeits his chance to eat any cookies—entrepreneurs who try to grab for too much money will probably lose the money they could have otherwise had. I think of "Mark," who was in the process of taking his company public one year prior to the dot-com crash in 2001. He had a company generating $7 million per year, but it had never really made a profit. Then a Web angle was concocted as a platform for significant expansion. A financing of $3 million was on the table, a projected post-listed market cap of $30 million. Mark would have had a paper share value of more than $10 million. Everyone admired Mark for being on the verge of reaping the rewards of his labor. But greed got the better of him. Despite the best advice from all corners to take the deal and begin growing the company, he thought he should be holding out for a better deal. The short of it is that he fell flat on his face: He pushed the underwriters too hard, the market changed, and the deal was off. His company subsequently went bankrupt, besieged by lawsuits and creditors. The sad part is, it didn't have to be that way.

6. Manage Risk

The key for entrepreneurs is to take calculated risks—after careful assessment. Successful entrepreneurs manage and reduce risk; short-term entrepreneurs ignore risk. The process of going public reveals entrepreneurs' differing approaches to risk. A successful public listing and subsequent growth has the potential to be extremely lucrative; however, the best approach is to be conservative within a risky process. Make sure everything is done properly and that contributors are rewarded accordingly. Pay the industry standard rates for key advisors such as lawyers, accountants, and underwriters. You may not like it, but that is the cost of the process. Rather than trying to nickel and dime everyone, plan for the costs properly from the outset and raise sufficient funds. Further, with respect to risk management, plan on the basis that things can take twice as long and be twice as expensive as you expect. Plan your corporate affairs with long lead times for regulatory approvals, and don't expect everyone else to be in a hurry just because you are. Reduce your risk through proper planning.

7. Keep Your Options Open

Your ability to make good decisions is, to some extent, dependent upon the number of worthwhile options you have available. Roger Fisher, author of *Getting to Yes*, calls this plan b the "Best Alternative to the Negotiated Agreement (BATNA).[17] His advice is to not make negotiating decisions without knowing your BATNA. Along those lines, an entrepreneur founder needs to understand what he needs to do to raise money and get support, and what will happen if he is not able to do so. One entrepreneur, a reputable educator, developed a system for online learning along with a Web technology that got people's attention. Unfortunately, the entrepreneur persisted in his vision for the global takeover of Web education instead of marketing his attractive Web engine technology. He kept persisting until he had run out of opportunities and was virtually bankrupt. He ended up choosing an alternative he had originally rejected, on worse terms than the ones initially offered.

8. You Are Not the Company

If the company cannot survive without you, then you don't have a real company. One entrepreneur was fond of telling me, "With me, everything is personal." In other words, he had to know everything that was happening in his company, all the time. The reality is that once you have an able management infrastructure in place, you should no longer be necessary. Entrepreneurs who have not made the transition to this forward-thinking role, and who are still immersed in details, put a cap on their growth.

These eight tips are simple reminders of some of the challenges faced by new ventures. I have seen each one of these pitfalls occur, and they can be the ruin of various companies or the track records of entrepreneurs.

Step 5 Recap

✓ Because most new ventures will need to raise money before they can generate internal cash flow to sustain their operations, a new venture's financing is critical to its survival.

✓ NowPublic demonstrates that crowd-powered companies can secure the backing of highly demanding venture capitalists.

✓ Entrepreneurs must be mindful of the dot-com bust and ensure they position themselves as a distinct and different investment proposition.

✓ Some of the most common sources of financing for an entrepreneur are: commercial banks, sub-debt lenders, angel investors, and venture capitalists (VCs).

✓ Discovery-driven strategic planning is a vital approach in the ever-changing environment of the new virtual marketplace.

✓ A crowdpreneur can sustain company growth by:
  ⇨ Accepting good advice.
  ⇨ Engaging in worthwhile introspection.
  ⇨ Managing one's ego.
  ⇨ Remembering the core.
  ⇨ Resisting greed.
  ⇨ Managing risk.
  ⇨ Keeping one's options open.
  ⇨ Making the company self-sustainable.

Feature

An Interview with Mike Sikorsky,
Cambrian House and the Path of Crowdsourcing

Crowdsourcing

Richard Goosen: When you started Cambrian House in February 2006, the term "crowdsourcing" had not yet been coined. When Jeff Howe invented it in June 2006, you immediately grabbed onto it. Why do you think that term—rather than preexisting phrases such as "mass collaboration" or "collective intelligence" took off?

Mike Sikorsky: Jeff is a brilliant communicator who was a smart enough guy to realize that there were many developments in the overall space of mass collaboration and collective intelligence—but no one had been able to give it a name that anyone could say out loud! Put simply, crowdsourcing is like outsourcing. If you phoned up your mom and told her that you are "harnessing collective intelligence," you wouldn't get far.

RG: There seems to be a lack of clarity as to how to define a crowdsourcing company. Some so-called crowdsourcing companies, such as istockphoto, appear to be more of a community rather than crowdsourcing site. Or, take Fluevog Shoes. They have crowdsourcing as one aspect of what they do, but at the same time they have been selling their shoes for 37 years. Do you think that the key issue, then, is whether a company can survive without the crowd?

MS: Yes, I think crowdsourcing companies are distinguished by being crowd-dependent. Without the crowds we're dead. It's imbedded into our DNA, versus being bolted on as a way to be more efficient in some aspect of a company's operations.

Website Launch

RG: Your Website had 50,000 hits within three days of launch—that's a phenomenal start right out of the gate. How did you do that?

MS: We have a great team with a lot of good ideas and we spent a lot of time worrying about the launch. We realized that we would need to get attention in the early phase of the launch of the site, otherwise we would not have a chance to win at crowdsourcing, because no one really knows how to win yet.

One general factor to our advantage is that people started reading about crowdsourcing.[1] Then, people heard about our approach because it was novel, and they decided we had a model they could believe in. We then began to build on this initial interest to create a viral interest that would spread rapidly.

One way to get a big leap out of the gate is to have something that is novel. The downside is that something novel also means your risk of failure increases. Cambrian House has always been either a grand slam at the World Series or a plane crashing down into everyone's den. The in-between was never really there for us.

So, I think that helped us be very careful and meticulous in planning our launch. We created a very specific launch plan that mapped out what to do on virtually every day for a six-month period. We sequenced the launch through a number of steps that helped us build up that momentum:

1. Even before we launched we started telling bloggers about the company.

2. We also ran a code for software developers at our site called "Cambrian Code" so that they could come and try to crack our puzzle.

3. Then we had the Google pizza event and that really added fuel to the fire.

4. Then when our Website went from Beta One to Beta Two, we had Beta special awards and the Website actually counted down and it took off at midnight that night and we then we launched the new site.

5. We built an entire story so that our community members could follow along with us on our journey.

I think one of the big mistakes most companies make when they launch is that they treat it like pulling a canvas off of a masterpiece someone has been sculpting for two years, and then expect everyone to flock to the site. In fact, companies are better off letting people join the journey along the way.

Innovation and the "Firsts"

RG: What would you summarize as the key "firsts" for Cambrian House?

MS: The most significant is that we are actually the first online company to be crowd-dependent. Without a crowd our whole business would not work. The crowd dictates where we put our capital.

Another first is to offer community ownership; each member who signs up on the site gets a share. We have set up a cooperative structure for people who are not our employees. We decided to offer community ownership because at present no one offers an incentive to crowds by way of equity participation. No one has invented that structure—it cost us almost $100,000 in legal fees to figure out how to do that. Even now a lot of our community members don't fully understand the structure, but we went ahead because we believe it is a new prototype.

RG: So if someone becomes a member and gets his one share, then you actually register him with your employee stock option plan? And do you notify him and tell him he has a share in the company, or do you actually send him a certificate or something?

MS: You can't actually do things like that, because shareholders are not actual employees. But what we have is a cooperative, which then has a relationship with the corporation: 1 percent of our equity and 1 percent of our yearly revenue is transferred over. In the cooperative there is a board of community members that then decides who deserves that compensation. So if they thought "John" was a great community member, then they can install a policy that says whoever has so many participation points get a certain percent of revenue and equity that year.

This approach is more complicated than, say, an employee stock-option plan. In those cases, employees are allocated a specific number of options for a particular period of time that they can exercise as long as they remain employed by the company. These plans are well understood and are easy to roll out. We are basically saying that we are trying to create something that is analogous to an employee stock-option plan. In short, we are trying to integrate crowdsourcing into our company, but it is not always easy to do.

Community Member Payouts

RG: How much money has been paid out to date for the contribution of ideas by community members?

MS: [There are two levels of payout: by Cambrian House for the contribution of the idea; and by community members who can contribute cash or services directly to the originators of the idea.] There has been a significant payout. The actual cash payout by Cambrian House has been around $10,000; we have received pre-orders and so we have to pay people out. The two guys that invented the idea for Gwabs are using their money to help them buy a house. Inside the community, the community members amongst themselves have paid out about $60 to $65,000 for various ideas. So, the crowd on its own has already eclipsed our Cambrian House payouts five- or six-fold.

RG: How does that work?

MS: Community members can crowdsource amongst themselves now. So let's just say you had an idea within the community, but Cambrian House didn't want to pay you royalty points. Any member can say to another, "hey, John, can I buy that idea off you for $1,000?" and you can say "sure." Then they transfer $1,000 and the idea ownership goes to somebody else. Or someone can say "hey, do you want to work on my project with me? I will pay you $5,000." So money is already transferring in our economy, which is totally wild.

RG: Why did you set up this two-track system?

MS: We have two branches [Prezzle and Gwabs] and a third popping alive, which is Greedy or Needy. This has happened within about two years [February 2006 to January 2008]. As a company, we are already maxed out! We likely can't get another idea going until late 2008 or early 2009. That is why members within the communities themselves are allowed to do whatever they want inside the ecosystem. That was one of the bottlenecks that we fixed when we moved from CH 1.0 to CH 2.0 [which then has become CH 3.0]. We allow the ecosystem to foster commerce. Members can exchange royalty points, money, idea ownership, and work. We tell them, "Go for it."

Discovery-Driven Planning—The Highs and Lows

RG: As you look back over two years of founding and operating a crowdsourcing company, what are some of the things that you are most proud of?

MS: First, I am most proud of the fact that we are a fairly small team sitting here in Calgary, Alberta, that became thought leaders in what I believe is going to be a part of every single company going forward. I think we are probably most proud of our ability to gain that thought leadership position and all the benefits that come with that. It's awesome. As a result of our thought leadership position we have been able to generate better contacts and opportunities than otherwise would have been possible.

Second, we were really proud of our launch. It is true that most companies have no idea if anyone cares about them. I was really proud that we could compel people to look at us because they thought it was meaningful.

The third thing for me, and the entire team, was to see the development of individuals in our community, For example, Andy Dollen, a member of our community, created the idea for Fundable Films. It changed his whole life. He was a young kid working in shipping and receiving for Magna Corp. [in Ontario]. He hated his job; his whole passion is films and entrepreneurship. He began online podcasting about his idea, building support, floating his ideas, and then he won our IdeaWarz Tournament. Now he has moved to Calgary from Ontario and has built this world-class board of people and secured venture capital financing. I do not know how his company will develop, but we have given him a great shot at success. The experience has changed his life. Every time I see him, I think it is awesome that we could help him get closer to achieving his dreams.

RG: As you look back over the past two years, what would you have done differently?

MS: I can bluntly say that there were some things that we were just dumb about. That's part of the entrepreneurial learning curve, however, particularly when you venture into uncharted territory such as crowdsourcing. The things that we screwed up the most were things that were to some extent forecast-able. We had the organizational design wrong in the beginning. I think we had it right on the community side, but wrong on the inside. It took us a year to a year and a half before we got it right. Because there are so many ideas in circulating in our ecosystem it is challenging to focus solely on the next big idea.

Then you throw in the fact that we are a really flat organization. What we realized—and this is the key learning principle—was that even though we wanted a flat hierarchy, we couldn't have a flat hierarchy of communication. We had to have a hierarchy around our communication. So, changing our hierarchy of communication and putting the right corporate structure around each of the opportunities was the saving grace for our company.

RG: You mention in your Water Cooler of March 2007 that Cambrian House needed to lay off a handful of people.

MS: That was painful. We had to contract because we were not able to create value in new projects. We think that we could have launched more companies if we would have had a different structure. Rather than having all these branches [that is, divisions] inside Cambrian House, we decided that a branch should secure its own investment and spin out its own corporate structure. The entity can get its own CEO and team. We had to scale back the number of opportunities we were looking at. That hurt culturally. Those are the situations that make you not want to be an entrepreneur, when you need to fire some of your friends.

From a company standpoint, what we had wrong there was the organizational design—the communication hierarchies. Eric Beinhocker, in his book *The Origin of Wealth,*[2] connects economic theory with social networking theory. He argues that mixing unpredictable decision-making with deep interconnections and flat hierarchy will create chaos. We experienced that. Of course we had unpredictable decision-making because there were so many ideas.

I take personal responsibility, too. I was probably the root of some of these organizational challenges because I led the organization to be fiercely aggressive. If I were to go back in time, I would have gone "medium" aggressive on some of our initiatives. I think we were too aggressive on building out the branches.

Transparency

RG: Transparency is a part of succeeding in a Web 2.0 world. From Cambrian House's standpoint, what have been the advantages and disadvantages of being transparent?

MS: With respect to disadvantages of transparency, the first is that you have to commit time to it. You don't achieve transparency at no cost. Perhaps we have been a bit extreme, but we originally went so far as to hire someone to film our internal meetings. Later on we simply used a Web cam; that was much more cost-effective. Today, we hire someone to film important meetings.

A second disadvantage is that transparency will reveal the ongoing challenges faced by a company as it goes through its development stages. When you are looking at a company, especially in a start-up phase, its organizational structure and lines of communication are not fully established. In the early days of Cambrian House, we were working hard at sorting out team chemistry, the organizational structure, and the appropriate amount of capital required. If someone looking at the company at that time didn't understand that a start-up company goes through early growth pains (regardless of how successful), [he or she] could interpret the early challenges in a negative way. Once again, the desire for transparency becomes an expense because we need to communicate to our users why change is normal for this phase of our company.

The benefit to being transparent is that it is a key way to connect with people. You can't compel people to commit deeply to your company; instead, transparency is a way of connecting with them.

RG: Is anything off-limits?

MS: From a cultural standpoint and because of our emphasis on communities, being highly confidential isn't actually the way to go. I don't think that will be an issue with us very often. [The only concern might relate to strategic-planning decisions that are in process.] There may be a few situations when confidentiality is necessary. For example, we may have potential partners in a pipeline and we can't reveal who they are or how many we are talking with. But asie from situations like that, our business and our business models are an open book and I can tell you everything.

Entrepreneurial Advice

RG: What advice do you have for entrepreneurs looking at Web 2.0 opportunities?

MS: The first piece of advice I give to anyone I ever meet is to "just do it and shut up." Thunder in the mouth and lightning in the hand—stop talking. No matter how many books you read, no matter how much stuff you're going to think about, if you don't decide to do it, you're already dead anyway. Action is much better. If you act, you're good.

Second, do not work on things that no one wants. I know that sounds so stupid, but the number of companies I know that build inventory no one wants to buy is so high it's phenomenal. That is why the crowd part to me is so powerful. If you can't get a crowd around your idea, how else are you going to get traction around your idea? I think if you just do it and not focus on building inventory, you're probably okay.

Third, you are probably going to screw up once or twice anyways, so you might as well start screwing up or blowing up whatever it is right now. I am not trying to evangelize this idea of not being prepared and not reading, but I also don't want to evangelize this idea of people who go away for 10 years before they want to start their company. It's like saving sex for old age. No matter how smart your team is, no matter how smart anything is, if you don't have a product that people want, you're going to have to dump whatever you're on and get that anyway. If you get those two things right and you're doing something that people like, the rest will work itself out.

Entrepreneurs are always worried that someone is going to steal their idea. Or they're worried that they're structuring their capital deals wrong. I tell them, "what are you worried about?"

Of course you want to plan, of course you want to think, of course you want to read, of course you want to do every possible thing that you can imagine to take the risk out of your company. But don't over-plan.

Paul Graham says, "my opinion is always best." So I always send anyone on coaching or trying to help out to *www.paulgraham.com*

and make them read his essays because he takes you through all these same points, but much better than I do.

Conclusion

Succeeding as a Crowdpreneur in the New Virtual Marketplace

There are five steps to succeeding as a crowdpreneur in the new virtual marketplace. I have summarized each of the steps at the end of each particular chapter. Rather than repeating all that again, and in the spirit of the opening of the book, the emphasis has been to apply entrepreneurial insights to the Web 2.0 and crowd-powered world. I prefer to impart new information in this conclusion that is based on extensive research into the cases of successful entrepreneurs.

For this reason, I turn to the insights of a colleague, Larry Farrell, who is a world leader in teaching entrepreneurial principles. A measure of his success is that Junior Achievement of America has incorporated his methodologies and insights into the teaching materials used by hundreds of thousands of elementary- and high-school students.

Farrell has distilled the insights he gained from 20 years of research into the actual practices of the world's leading entrepreneurs, into four common characteristics of successful start-ups. Any entrepreneur can use this basic framework to achieve initial success, and any corporate management team can use the framework to instill growth in a business. Farrell's teaching track record indicates that clients the world over find his analysis compelling.

First, the entrepreneur must have a clear "sense of mission," which Farrell says includes both "what" the mission is and "how" the entrepreneur is going to achieve it. This begins with tailoring the company's product to a particular market, which Farrell calls having a product/market strategy. Next is how a person can achieve that strategy: "Entrepreneurs have to get this right. Concentrating your energies on becoming the best in the world at one or two key things will give you powerful, competitive advantages."[1] He further states, "When your values directly support your product/market strategy, hang on! It's the most powerful way ever invented to energize a group of individuals to achieve a common purpose. That's why having a powerful sense of mission is the first entrepreneurial practice."[2] The history of IBM shows that a strong sense of mission can fuel company growth, and that a loss of mission can derail a company later in its life cycle.

Farrell explains how IBM, "Big Blue," was founded in 1914 by Thomas Watson, Sr. Watson infused staff with his mission through a pithy set of values: customer service, respect for the individual, and superior effort in all tasks. Watson saw IBM's competitive advantage as outstanding customer service, whatever the product. For years, its corporate advertising simply declared, "IBM Means Service." IBM crowed that because of this service emphasis, 95 percent of all product ideas came from its customers.[3] Interestingly enough, these values were so pervasive that they were not written down until 1963, when Thomas Watson, Jr., recorded them—50 years after his father founded the company. The founder's leadership and personal embodiment of core principles had kept those values alive. IBM was a great organization for a long time. Today it still ranks highly in sales and profits on the Fortune 500 list, but, Farrell notes, "it's fair to say they're past their peak, some 20 years into the down side of their life cycle."[4] IBM's original mission and resulting entrepreneurial zeal evaporated in the 1980s, when it nearly collapsed. In the 1990s, despite some revival, IBM still was a lumbering, slow-moving behemoth in an area that was overtaken by innovative high-growth competitors. Company growth is propelled by a strong sense of mission, such as IBM had in the early stage of its life cycle.

Second, the entrepreneur needs to have a clear "customer/product vision." In practical terms, this means the entrepreneur must be very clear about who is going to buy the product and why. Farrell writes, "The single most crucial vision all entrepreneurs must have is a clear picture of a specific set of customers who need and will pay for a specific set of products and services. Nothing could be more basic to the entrepreneur."[5] Farrell makes a critical point that a successful entrepreneur is almost always both a "product person" and a "customer person." He or she is a make-and-sell craftsman with the classic customer/product vision of an entrepreneur. Farrell recounts the story of Walt Disney, the "greatest product creator in the history of the entertainment business"[6]: Disney produced the first talking cartoon in 1928 (*Steamboat Willie*), the first feature-length animated cartoon in 1937 (*Snow White*), the first stereophonic movie in 1940 (*Fantasia*), and the world's first 360-degree projection at Disneyland in 1955. In television, Disney also created "The Wonderful World of Disney," the longest-running prime-time series ever (1954 to 1983). He opened Disneyland in 1955, and before he died in 1966, he laid the groundwork for Walt Disney World in Florida. What was his magic? According to Farrell, the real "magic" of Walt Disney is simple: "He was a product expert and a customer expert at the same time. A scientist and a salesman. An unbeatable combination."[7] Farrell explains, "The trick, then, is to become passionately expert on your own products and customers. After all, they are the two most important ideas in business."[8]

Third, an entrepreneur needs to deploy "high-speed innovation." Farrell states, "There are two golden rules for high-speed innovation: First, you and your people must see innovation as an absolute necessity in the business; and, second, there must be a high sense of urgency to take action and implement new ideas. We call it the necessity to invent and the freedom to act."[9]

He notes, "The evidence is indisputable that young, entrepreneurial companies can, and regularly do, simply beat the socks off their larger, more mature competitors. And almost always, their number-one competitive advantage is that they move faster and they're more creative than their larger rivals."[10] Further, "I have never known an entrepreneur who operated without pretty high levels of emotion and without a strong sense of urgency."[11] The entrepreneur needs to act swiftly before the competitive landscape changes and the windows of opportunity close.

Farrell tells the tale of Larry Hillblom and the founding of DHL. Hillblom was a young law student in northern California who did freelance courier work on weekends, carrying packages across the Pacific on 20-hour flights. He scratched out an idea for an international courier company with two of his law school friends who were also freelance couriers. They formed DHL (Dalsey, Hillblom, and Lynn) and began to offer overnight delivery, but they needed an international network of offices immediately. The result: "They opened an amazing 120 country offices in the first 10 years of DHL's existence (1972 to 1982), which is still the fastest international expansion of any company in history."[12] In the process, Hillblom created a company that today generates approximately $15 billion in revenue. Of course, subsequent international courier companies have been created, such as FedEx, but the rise of DHL was rooted in almost unbelievable high-speed innovation. High-speed innovation was necessary to create the infrastructure to deliver the service represented by DHL. Entrepreneurial success requires acting immediately and decisively in response to an opportunity in the marketplace.

Fourth, an entrepreneur must have "self-inspired behavior"—to spur on himself and his employees. The entrepreneur is the engine, and his company is the vehicle. Farrell clarifies: "To start your own business, *you* have to be self-inspired. Then, to grow your enterprise, you have to learn to inspire others. That is why mastering the final entrepreneurial practice, *self-inspired behavior*, is the underpinning of all entrepreneurial success."[13] He goes on, "To successfully grow beyond the proverbial one-man shop, some enterprising, self-inspired behavior needs to be instilled in the employees. Inspiring yourself is laudable—that's where it has to start—but inspiring 10, or a 100, or even thousands of workers is the real trick."[14] Farrell cites the example of Soichiro Honda, founder of the Honda Motor Company, whom he calls "hands down, the most interesting Japanese entrepreneur of the 20th century."[15] The son of a blacksmith, with only a third-grade education, Honda built a company famous for its attention to customers and its efficient system, through which workers (whether in Japan or in the United States) created highly competitive cars. His death in 1991 produced a wide outpouring of grief among employees worldwide. Soichiro Honda was not only a highly self-motivated individual, but he also inspired his entire organization.

To conclude, these four essential characteristics of an entrepreneur are equally important for success as a crowdpreneur in the new virtual marketplace. The Web 2.0 world is still the beginning stages of the Internet, a technology that will continue to change our world dramatically. The best way to stay in tune with developments is to be part of them—engage in the Internet world, and keep the principles of entrepreneurship in mind. Let this book remind you of important steps as you explore the possibilities in this growing sector.

You won't become a crowdpreneur overnight, but with enough exposure to the Internet environment you will begin to understand the Internet's nuances more clearly. In most books this point would be the end—the finish line. In this book, however, you're at the starting point. Now it's your chance to put the principles in this book to work. You may want to visit our Website, *www.crowdpreneur.com*, to learn more about entrepreneurship in the Web 2.0 sphere and interact with other readers.

Appendix A

Introduction to Crowdpreneur Networks Inc.

Crowdpreneur Networks, Inc. is based in Vancouver, British Columbia, and Palo Alto, California. The company focuses on providing insight and analysis of crowd-powered entrepreneurship. The company's Website (*www.crowdpreneur.com*) maintains an online journal and a blog for information regarding the topic. The online journal features interviews with top thought leaders and businesspeople in the field. Rick Goossen is the founder and CEO of Crowdpreneur.

The company has coined the term "crowdpreneur" as amethod of providing focus for businesspeople wishing to pursue opportunities within the Web 2.0 world of crowd power. Although crowd power can be deployed in various ways, this term interates entrepreneurship and crowd involvement.

The Website also provides a vehicle for ongoing dialogue with *e-Preneur* readers and others who are interested in the topic. In the spirit of crowd power, I am interested in obtaining ideas and feedback.

Rick Goossen
Founder and CEO
Crowdpreneur Networks, Inc.
Vancouver, British Columbia, and Palo Alto, California

Introduction to The Centre for Entrepreneurial Leaders

The Centre for Entrepreneurial Leaders (CEL) (*www .eleaders.org*) is based at the School of Business, Trinity Western University (TWU), in the greater Vancouver area of BC, Canada. TWU (*www.twu.ca*) was established in 1962 and is a nonprofit Christian liberal arts university with approximately 4,000 students; the School of Business (*www.twu.ca/business*), established in 1975, has an enrollment of over 500 students in eight specializations (including entrepreneurship).

The CEL is managed by its director, Rick Goossen, and oversight is provided by TWU. The CEL is fortunate to have the involvement and support of its "Advisors," who are prominent and successful entrepreneurs. The present Advisors to the CEL are: Ross Colello, Ken Ewert, Eugene Kaulius, Rudy Loewen, Grant Ohman, Franco Papalia, Terry Smith, Roy Stevenson, Cameron Stromsmoe, Brian Tieszen, and Andrew Westlund.

The CEL was founded in 2007 by Rick Goossen. The vision of the CEL is to be a leading international center for education, advancement, and research of values-oriented entrepreneurial leadership. The mission of the CEL is achieved in five ways: research, teaching, publications, organizing community events, and participating in conferences. As part of its mandate, the CEL supports the research initiatives undertaken by its director. As a result, the CEL provided support for the research related to the publication of *e-Preneur*.

The CEL is involved in three key promotional activities each year. It organizes and hosts an Annual Entrepreneur Forum that is among the largest of its kind in North America. The 3rd Annual Entrepreneur Forum in November 2007 featured one of North America's leading motivational speakers, Peter Legge, addressing a full house of entrepreneurs from around the world. In addition the CEL publishes an annual collection of interviews of successful entrepreneurs under the title *Entrepreneurial Leaders: Reflections on Faith at Work*; Vol. 4 will be available in September 2008. Lastly, the CEL inaugurated a visiting professor program in 2008 to bring a leading international academic to Vancouver to address issues related to faith, ethics, and business. The first visiting professor was Dr. Richard Higginson, Ridley Hall Foundation, Cambridge, United Kingdom.

Rick Goossen

Founder and Director
Centre for Entrepreneurial Leaders
School of Business
Trinity Western University

Notes

Introduction:

1. Grossman, "Time's Person."
2. Ibid.
3. Gladwell 280.
4. Tapscott & Williams, 13.
5. Originally published in 1841 under the title *Memoirs of Extraordinary Popular Delusions*. Foreword by Andrew Tobias.
6. Mackay, xviii.
7. Ibid., 14.
8. Ibid., 14-5.
9. Ibid., 92.
10. Ibid., 93.
11. Ibid., 94.
12. Ibid., viii.
13. Rheingold, xii.
14. Ibid., xix.
15. Surowiecki, xiii.
16. Ibid., xv.
17. Ibid., xviii.
18. Ibid., 11.
19. Another similar term is "user-centered innovation," which is favored by Eric von Hippel of MIT.
20. *http://en.wikipedia.org/wiki/Open_Innovation.* Viewed March, 2008.
21. *www.leapinghare.co.uk/help/glossary.html#O.* Viewed March, 2008.
22. *http://en.wikipedia.org/wiki/Mass_collaboration.* Viewed March, 2008.

23. "Abstract" from MIT Communications Forum, October 4, 2007. Viewed at *www.web.mit.edu/comm-forum/forums/collective_intelligence.html.*

26. Tim O'Reilly, telephone interview with author, September 5, 2007.

27. Ibid.

28. Ibid.

29. "Crowd Clout." *www.trendwatching.com/trends/crowdclout.htm.* Viewed March, 2008.

30. Howe, Jeff "The Rise"

31. A good overview is provided by Alsever, Jennifer. "What is Crowdsourcing?" BNET Briefing. *www.bnet.com/2403-13241_23-52961.htmal.* Viewed May 16, 2007.

32. Catone, Josh. "Crowdsourcing"

33. Jeff Howe, telephone interview with author, August 31, 2007.

35. "Crowd Power." *www.nowpublic.com/newsroom/tools/crowd_power.* Viewed March, 2008

36. Foot, *Boom,* 14.

37. Ibid., 19.

38. Beaumont, Claudine. "TechCrunch"

Profile of Tim O'Reilly:

1. Interview of Tim O'Reilly by the author by telephone, September 5, 2007.

2. Network effects become significant after a certain subscription percentage has been achieved, called critical mass. At the critical mass point, the value obtained from the good or service is greater than or equal to the price paid for the good or service. As the value of the good is determined by the user base, this implies that after a certain number of people have subscribed to the service or purchased

the good, additional people will subscribe to the service or purchase the good due to the positive utility: price ratio.

Source: *http://en.wikipedia.org/wiki/Network_effect.*

3. O'Reilly interview.

4. O'Reilly, Tim. "What is Web 2.0" September 30, 2005.

5. O'Reilly interview.

6. Ibid.

7. Ibid.

8. Bricklin, Dan. "The Cornucopia" Viewed October 1, 2007.

9. O'Reilly interview.

10. O'Reilly, Tim. "Emerson and Oliver" (September 2, 2007).

11. See "What is Web 2.0."

12. O'Reilly interview.

13 Ibid.

14. Hedlund, Mark. "Making the web" July 25, 2007.

15. O'Reilly interview.

16. *www.oreilly.com/about/.*

17. O'Reilly interview.

18. Maker Faire is a two-day, family-friendly event that celebrates arts, crafts,engineering,science projects, and the Do-It-Yourself (DIY) mindset. It's for creative, resourceful folks who like to tinker and love to make things. We call them Makers. See *www.makerfaire.com.*

Step 1: The Entrepreneurial Lens

1. McGirt, Ellen. "Hacker.", 74.

2. McCarthy, Caroline. "Microsoft acquire."

3. Allison, Kevin. "Cisco's chief places," 13.

4. See Clayton Christensen's *The Innovator's Dilemma: The Revolutionary Book that Will Change the Way You Do Business* (1997).

5. Schumpeter, Joseph. *Capitalism,* 83.

6. Farrell, *Getting Entrepreneurial!,* 59.

7. Ibid., 71.

8. Ibid., 13.

9. Jeffrey Timmons, telephone interview with the author, November 17, 2004.

10. Timmons, Jeffrey, and Stephen Spinelli, *New Venture,* 47.

11. Ibid.

12. Ibid., 56.

13. Jeffrey Timmons interview.

14. Ibid.

15. Timmons and Spinelli, *New Venture,* 67.

16. Ibid., 62.

17. Ibid., 56.

18. "Top Ten Crowdsourcing Companies." August 1, 2006.

Company Profile: Cambrian House

1. Surowiecki, 28.

2. Mike Sikorsky, telephone interview with the author, January 18, 2008.

3. Cambrian House "Executive Summary." (Undated, but received in April 2007), 1.

4. Cambrian House Water Cooler (Monthly Investor Update), April 2006.

5. Ibid., May 2006.

6. Ibid., August 2006.

7. Spring 2007 Investor Presentation.

8. Ibid.

9. *www.cambrianhouse.com.*

10. Ibid.

11. Cambrian House Water Cooler, June 2006.

12. See, for example, Om Malik's blog entry titled "Web 2.0, Community and the Commerce Conundrum," October 18, 2005. *http://gigaom.com.*

13. Cambrian House Water Cooler, April 2006.

14. Ibid., August 2007.

15. Ibid., August 2007.

16. Ibid., September 2007.

17. Ibid., March 2006.

18. Ibid., May 2006.

29. Ibid., 2007.

Step 2: Opportunities Through Innovation

1. Friedman, Thomas L. *The World is Flat: The Globalized World in the Twenty-First Century*. London: Penguin Books, 2005.

2. Sikorsky interview.

3. Ibid.

4. Barringer and Ireland, *Entrepreneurship*, 39.

5. Timmons and Spinelli, *New Venture Creation*, 11–12.

6. McCraw, *Prophet*, 495.

7. Ibid., 3.

8. Ibid., 496.

9. Ibid., 259. Quoted from *Business Cycles: A Theoretical, Historical and Statistical Analysis of the Capitalist Process*. New York: Macmillan, 1939.

10. Drucker, Peter F. *Innovation and Entrepreneurship*, 277–8.

11. Ibid., 280.

12. Ibid., 285.

13. Ibid.

14. Ibid., 317.

15. Ibid., 318.

16. Ibid., 321.

17. Ibid., 322.

18. Ibid., 285.

19. Ibid., 345.

20. Ibid.

21. Ibid., 350.

22. Ibid., 357.

23. Christensen, *The Innovator's Dilemma*, xv.

24. Ibid.

25. Ibid., xvi.

26. Ibid.

27. Ibid.

28. Ibid., xxiii.

29. Ibid., xxiv.

30. Ibid., xxv.

31. Ibid., xxvi.

32. Ibid., xxvii.

33. Ibid., 181.

34. Ibid., 182.

35. Christensen, *The Innovator's Solution*, 227–9.

36. For further information see chapter titled "Rita Gunther McGrath: The Entrepreneurial Mindset and Discovery-Driven Strategy," 97–110, in Goossen, Richard J., *Entrepreneurial Excellence: Profit from the Best Ideas of the Experts* (2007).

37. Rita Gunther McGrath, telephone interview with the author, March 29, 2005.

38. Ibid.

39. McGrath, *The Entrepreneurial Mindset*, 236.

40. Ibid.

41. Ibid., 237.

42. Ibid., 238.

43. Ibid., 241.

44. Ibid.

45. Ibid, 242.

46. Ibid, 243.

47. Ibid.

48. McGrath interview.

49. Christensen, *The Innovator's Dilemma*, 260.

50. Sawyer, Keith, Group Genius, 14-7.

51. Ibid., 191-3.

52. Taylor and LaBarre, *Mavericks at Work*, 118.

53. Ibid., 120.

54. Ibid., 121

55. Ibid.

56. Ibid., 123.

57. Ibid., 124.

58. Rushkoff, *Get Back in the Box*, 19.

59. Ibid., 195.

60. Ibid., 197-8.

61. Ibid., 223.

62. Ibid., 228.

63. Putnam, *Bowling Alone,* 16.

64. Ibid., 19.

65. Ibid., 27.

66. Ibid., 169.

67. "S-Commerce." October 2006.

Interview With Jeff Howe

1. See Jeff's blog at *http://crowdsourcing.typepad.com*.

2. See pages 63 and 190.

3. See also *www-users.cs.york.ac.uk/~susan/cyc/l/law.htm*.

4. See *http://services.alphaworks.ibm.com/manyeyes/home*.

5. See discussion of *www.InnoCentive.com* on p. 146.

Step 3: Feasibility Analysis of the Opportunity

1. The general information for this introductory section, unless otherwise noted, is from *www.threadless.com*.

2. *http://blog.guykawasaki.com/2007/06/ten_questions_w.html*. Viewed March, 2008.

3. *http://zero.newassignment.net/filed/threadless_interview _jeffrey_kalmikoff_ chief_creat*.

4. Ibid.

5. Barringer and Ireland, *Entrepreneurship* 76-7.

6. Ibid., 142-3.

7. Ibid., 144.

8. Ibid., 148.

9. Ibid., 83.

10. Ibid., 85.

11. Jeff Howe interview.

12. Catone, Josh. "Crowdsourcing" March 22, 2007.

13. Mike Tippett, interview with the author, Vancouver, BC, August 24, 2007.

14. Ibid.

15. Ibid.

16. Ibid.

Step 4: Developing an Effective Crowd-Power Business Model

1. Lam, Kempton and Nisan, Gabbay. "iStockphoto Case Study" November 26, 2006.

2. Ibid.

3. *www.istockphoto.com.* Viewed February 4, 2008.

4. "2006 Fast 50" Viewed October 2, 2007.

5. Barringer and Ireland, *Entrepreneurship*, 163.

6. Ibid., 165.

7. For a good overview of Web business models, see: Rappa, Michael, "Business Models on the Web," *Managing the Digital Enterprise*. From *http://digitalenterprise.org/models/models.html.* Viewed January 2, 2008.

8. Chris Breikss interview with the author, Vancouver, BC, December 14, 2007

9. Ibid.

10. Ibid.

11. Ibid.

12. Ibid.

13. Ibid.

14. Ibid.

15. Cambrian House, PowerPoint presentation.

16. Executive Summary (undated).

17. Ibid.

18. Sikorsky interview.

19. Cambrian House Water Cooler, May 2006.

20. Ibid., October 2007.

Company Profile: Fluevog Shoes

1. Stephen Bailey, interview with the author, Vancouver, BC, June 22, 2007.

2. John Fluevog interview, cited in Goossen, Richard J. *The Christian Entrepreneur: Insights from the Marketplace, Vol. II*, (2006), 171.

3. "Top Ten Crowdsourcing Companies." From *http://innovationzen.com/blog/2006/08/01/top-10-crowdsourcing-companies*.

4. *www.fluevog.com/files_2/voting.html*.

5. Ibid.

6. *www.fluevog.com/flueshots/main.php*.

7. *www.fluevog.com/files_2/os-1.html*.

8. Bailey interview.

9. *www.fluevog.com/files_2/os-1.html*.

10. Bailey interview.

11. Ibid.

12. Ibid.

Step 5: Financing and Growing the Company

1. "NowPublic.com Closes" July 30, 2007.

2. "Our Approach," Rho Ventures.

3. Ibid.

4. Lee-Young, Joanne, "News site secures" E31.

5. Sikorsky interview.

6. Ibid.

7. Ibid.

8. Ibid.

9. Ibid.

10. Ibid.

11. Cambrian House Water Cooler, May 2006.

12. Sikorsky interview.

13. *www.CambrianHouse.com.*

14. Cambrian House Water Cooler, March 2007.

15. Ibid., April 2007.

16. Ibid.

17. The "BATNA" concept is discussed throughout the book: Fisher, R. and, W. Ury *Getting to Yes: Negotiating Agreement Without Giving In* (2nd ed). New York: Penguin, 1991.

Interview With Mike Sikorsky

1. In June 2006, after Jeff Howe's *Wired Magazine* article.

2. Beinhocker, Eric D. *The Origin of Wealth: The Radical Remaking of Economics and What it Means for Business and Society.* Whitby, Ontario. McGraw-Hill Ryerson, 2007.

Conclusion: Succeeding as a Crowdpreneur in the New Virtual Marketplace

1. Farrell, *Getting Entrepreneurial!*, 43.

2. Ibid., 12—13.

3. Ibid., 39.

4. Larry Farrell, interview with the author, December 9, 2004.

5. Farrell, *Getting Entrepreneurial!*, 59.

6. Ibid., 71.

7. Ibid., 75.

8. Ibid., 13.

9. Ibid.

10. Ibid., 108.

11. Ibid., 125.

12. Ibid., 122.

13. Ibid., 14.

14. Ibid., 150—1.

15. Ibid., 176.

Bibliography

Crowdpreneur Links

www.adaptivepath.com/ideas/essays/archives/000385.php

Ajax: a New Approach to Web Applications (article by Jesse James Garrett)

www.backofmyhand.com

A crowd-powered Website in which people familiar with an area on a map select it, point out favorite (and worst) routes, and give more info about the best locations.

www.billionswithzeroknowledge.com/index.php?tag=jeff-howe

Crowdsourcing blog as part of Interviews, Stories, and Tales from a Canadian technology entrepreneur… "Crowdsourcing or Community Production – An Interview with Hugh McGuire from Librivox."

http://www.businessinnovationfactory.com/

The Business Innovation Factory is a community of innovators collaborating to explore and test better ways to deliver value. BIF Members and Partners explore business model innovation through a series of experiences designed to get ideas off of the white board and onto the ground as quickly and cost effectively as possible.

www.businessweek.com/innovate/content/jul2006/ id20060713_755844.htm?chan=search

Crowdsourcing: Consumers as Creators (article by Paul Boutin)

www.businessweek.com/magazine/content/06_39/b4002422 .htm?chan=search

Crowdsourcing: Milk the Masses for Inspiration (article by Jessi Hempel)

http://buzzcanuck.typepad.com/agentwildfire/2007/10/7- questions-wit.html.

Interview with Sami Viitamaki about the Crowdsourcing FLIRT model.

http://conferences.oreillynet.com/cs/et2005/view/e_sess/6336

    O'Reilly Emerging Technology Conference 2005: About, Tutorials, and so on. (PowerPoint presentation also available)

www.crowdsource.wordpress.com

    A crowdsourcing directory

www.crowdsourceit.net

    A site for information and links relating to crowdsourcing.

http://crowdsourcingdirectory.com/

    A helpful directory of crowdsourcing companies in various industries.

http://crowdsourcing.typepad.com

    Jeff Howe's blog. The following (aside from the definition, which appears on the left sidebar) is a list of blog entries:

        Definition of Crowdsourcing

        Calling all Academics: Getting a Head Count

        Reading, Writing and Arithmetic

        When Crowdsourcing Isn't…

        Neo Neologisms

        A Million Heads…

        A Million Doubts…

        The Prolific Crowd

        Curating by Flickr

        Diversity of the Crowd: Part I & II

        Creativity of the Crowd

        Andrew Keen's *Cult of the Amateur*

        Digital Sharecropping: Mesh takes on Crowdsourcing

        Commercializing Community (How to)

        Crowdsourcing: The Book

        Cambrian House

Assignment Zero… They Like Us, They Really Like Us (Except these guys)

As Long as We're on the Subject

Faces in the Crowd Interview Series

Second Life, and Gwyneth Llewelyn

Crowdfunding Political Candidates

http://crowdsourcing.wordpress.com/category/crowdsourcing/
Posts on Crowdsourcing.

http://crowdspirit.com/
Website dedicated to crowdsourcing ideas for new electronic devices. The site itself looks a little sketchy in terms of credibility.

http://en.wikipedia.org/wiki/crowdsourcing
Wikipedia on Crowdsourcing

http://en.wikipedia.org/wiki/mass_collaboration
Wikipedia on Mass Collaboration

www.foundmagazine.com
A magazine calling to the crowd for "findings."

http://garysteinblog.blogspot.com/2006/07/crowdsourcing-links.html
Gary Stein's blog about crowdsourcing, with comments from crowdsourcing start-ups.

http://getsatisfaction.com/
Crowd-powered customer service for any company or product

www.igniterealtime.org/
The community site for users and developers of open source Real Time Communications projects. (run by Jive Software: www.jivesoftware.com)

www.internetnews.com
Searching for the Wisdom of the Crowd (Article by Nicholas Carlson)

www.internetnews.com/bus-news/print.php/3614451
>For AOL Founder, 'RevolutionHealth' is Now

www.internetnews.com/bus-news/article.php/3672976
>Does AOL Video Answer Speculation?

www.internetnews.com/bus-news/print.php/3623686
>Making Money for the Flickr Flock?

www.internetnews.com/bus-news/print.php/3625541
www.istockphoto.com
>Crowd-powered stock photography site

www.jjg.net/ia/
>*The Elements of User Experience* (see also under Books), by Jesse James Garrett. The original chart that inspired the subsequent book. Chapter excerpt also available. Discusses websites as user interfaces, and the logic behind them.

www.longtail.com/the_long_tail/2007/02/the_one_thing_e.html.
>Author Chris Anderson's blog. This entry: The One Thing Everybody Forgets About "We Media."

www.lulu.com/en/community/
>An online print community creating books improved by crowdsourced advice and crowdsourced interest.

www.mass-customization.de/
>Frank Piller's Website on Mass Customization, Customer Integration, and Open Innovation.

www.mechanicalturk.com
>Offers small change for simple and somewhat mindless tasks that people can do better than computers. Part of Amazon.

www.mindquarry.com
>An open source collaborative software platform for file sharing and harnessing collective intelligence through the Internet.

http://money.cnn.com/magazines/business2/
>Business 2.0 Magazine home page—Interesting links and articles

http://money.cnn.com/magazines/business2/business2_archive/
2006/09/01/8384338/index.htm?postversion=2006091105
Business 2.0 Article: Suddenly Everything's Coming Up Widgets
(by Om Malik)

www.nytimes.com/2007/09/09/business/yourmoney/09second.html
New York Times article: Even in a Virtual World, Stuff Matters (by
Ed Regan), Published Sept. 9, 2007.

www.news.com/8301-10784_3-6095563-7.html?tag=tb
Can "crowdsourcing" be slave labor? (article by Mike Yamamoto,
Tech News Blog on CNET news)

http://nexuspress.pbwiki.com/
Wiki press release for the Web 2.0 conference in Singapore.

www.no-spec.com/
A site against 'spec work' (crowdsourced creative services—free
pitching, freeloading, and so on).

http://openad.net/
A site where companies can browse through advertising ideas and
pick their favorites.

www.openarchitecturenetwork.org/
An open-source architecture site that seeks to meet global chal-
lenges and improve living standards around the world. (Led by
Architecture for Humanity)

www.openbusiness.cc/2006/04/25/
People Inside and Web 2.0: An Interview with Tim O'Reilly

www.openoffice.org
An open-source alternative to MS Office.

www.oreilly.com
What is Web 2.0? (by Tim O'Reilly, 2005)

www.oreilly.com/lpt/a/6228
Google Uses Crowdsourcing to Create Maps in India

www.oreilly.com/archives/2007/08/google_uses_cro.html

www.oreillynet.com

Get Your Hands Dirty! (Article by Tim O'Reilly, 2005)
www.oreillynet.com/lpt/a/5573

O'Reilly Network Weblogs: Ask Jeff Bezos, Adam Bosworth,John D…
www.oreillynet.com/lpt/wlg/5630

Pick the Hat to Fit the Head (Tim O'Reilly, 2004)
http://tim.oreilly.com/lpt/a/5372

Open Source Guru Tim O'Reilly Loves his G4! (Simon Hayes)
www.macdirectory.com/newmd/mac/PAGES/NTRVU/ TimOReilly

Technology and Tools of Change (Tim O'Reilly, 2004)
http://tim.oreilly.com/lpt/a/5095

Open Source Paradigm Shift (Tim O'Reilly, 2004)
http://tim.oreilly.com/lpt/a/4868

State of the Computer Book Market (Tim O'Reilly,2004)
http://tim.oreilly.com/lpt/a/4672

Interview: O'Reilly and Associates (by Alain Buret,2004)
http://archive.fosdem.org/2004/index/interviews/ interviews_oreilly

The Future of Technology and Proprietary Software (Tim O'Reilly, 2003)
http://tim.oreilly.com/lpt/a/4488

Amazon and Open Source (O'Reilly, 2004)
www.oreilly.com/lpt/a/4617

Tim O'Reilly Interview, Part 1: Web 2.0
www.readwriteweb.com/archives/tim_oreilly_int.php

www.patientslikeme.com/
Crowdsourced medical advice, stories, and treatment ideas

http://www.ponoko.com/
A site where you can create design plans plus cost estimates for everything from earrings to furniture and make and sell your products in an online store.

www.readwriteweb.com/archives/crowdsourcing_million_heads.php
Crowdsourcing: A Million Heads is Better than One (article by Josh Catone, with comments. This article was cited and analyzed by Jeff Howe in his blog.)

http://redmonk.com/
The first analyst firm built on open source operation principles. It provides high-quality research at no cost, to even the gap between rich and poor.

http://www.samiviitamaki.com/2007/02/16/
Sami Viitamaki's blog on his FLIRT model of Crowdsourcing. (in print, see back of blue binder)

www.secondlife.com
Online virtual world in which avatars (virtual people) interact in real-world scenarios. Jeff Howe's original ideal example of crowdsourcing.

www.senokian.com/
Company that advises other companies with regard to using the Open Source concept.

http://services.alphaworks.ibm.com/manyeyes/home
IBM's launch of a crowd-empowered information visualizer with the goal of "democratizing" visualization and data analysis.

www.singaporeseen.stomp.com.sg/index.aspx
Online crowd-sourced news/news gossip in Singapore.

www.smartmobs.com

A site focused on the mobile "mob" revolution. Contains a blog about recent developments in crowdsourcing (though not specifically termed that) and information about the book *Smart Mobs* by Howard Rheingold. Book summary also available on site.

http://www.socialmediatoday.com/

"The web's best thinkers on social media and Web 2.0" – a moderated online business community for social media bloggers, marketers, PR, and media professionals, with a list of featured bloggers.

www.socialtext.net/wikinomics/index.cgi?introduction_to_the_wikinomics_playbook

Wikinomics mass collaboration book, as a response to the original *Wikinomics* book by Don Tapscott.

http://www.spigit.com/homepage

A site combining mathematics, technology, and subject matter experts to add relevance to online communities, for the purpose of elevating good ideas and good people.

www.springwise.com/style_design/crowdsourcing_graphic_design

Springwise: Crowdsourcing Graphic Design – and the backlash of complaints from professional graphic designers.

http://swarmsketch.com

Crowdsourced doodling. Most of it looks like a giant scribble, but people appear to enjoy it. You can draw a line and rate other people's lines to make them more or less prominent in the drawing.

www.teachthepeople.com/app/ttp

Teach the People is "the world's first social community and content networking service equipped with tools and features for the flexible sharing of knowledge." Also called "the People Powered University."

www.thedigitalmovement.org/web20/
> A young organization from Singapore seeking to build up a global community of Web 2.0 leaders. It was the organizer behind Nexus 2007, the first major Web 2.0 conference in Singapore.

www.theory.isthereason.com/?p=1586
> Speaker Kevin Lim's detailed review of the Nexus 2007 conference

www.threadless.com
> Site featuring open source clothing design

www.trendwatching.com/trends/2007top5.htm
> On the Radar for 2007 (Top Consumer Trends)

www.triggerstreet.com
> Short film, screenplay, or script creation that is open to the public for crowd-sourced editing, funding, and rating.

http://turkers.castingwords.com
> Crowdsourcing transcription from digital audio files to word documents. Same idea and company as Mechanical Turk.

www.tutorom.com/
> collaborative e-learning: "Access thousands of lessons or use our tools to create and control access to your own courses. Collaborate with colleagues…"

http://www.twine.com/
> A revolutionary new way to share, organize, and find information. Use Twine to better leverage and contribute to the collective intelligence of your friends, colleagues, groups and teams. Twine ties it all together.

http://www.webex.com/partners/webex-connect.html
> Collaboration enabling: "Combine leading business process applications and contextual data with real-time WebEx collaborative applications, making truly innovative solutions available on demand. Take advantage of this opportunity to create and deliver next generation business services and workflow that bridge the gap between

on-premise and SaaS applications—making it easy for knowledge workers across the globe to collaborate and get work done."

http://wethink.wikia.com/wiki/Main_Page

A wiki examining Charles Leadbeater's upcoming book about the rise of mass, collaborative creativity.

www.wired.com

Original Crowdsourcing Article:

The Rise of Crowdsourcing
www.wired.com/wired/archive/14.06/crowds_pr.html

The Trend Spotter: About Tim O'Reilly
http://wired-vig.wired.com/wired/archive/13.10/ oreilly_pr.html

Web Timeline:

We are the Web
www.wired.com/wired/archive/13.08/tech_pr.html

The Whiz Kid: Marc Andreessen (1995)
www.wired.com/wired/archive/13.08/1995_pr.html

The Guides: Jerry Yang (1996)
www.wired.com/wired/archive/13.08/1996_pr.html

The Merchant King: Jeff Bezos (1997)
www.wired.com/wired/archive/13.08/1997_pr.html

The Microsoft Slayer: David Boies (1998)
www.wired.com/wired/archive/13.08/1998_pr.html

The Icon: Rob Smiley (1999)
www.wired.com/wired/archive/13.08/1999_pr.html

The Music Swapper: Shawn Fanning (2000)
www.wired.com/wired/archive/13.08/2000_pr.html

The Stock Picker: Mary Meeker (2001)
www.wired.com/wired/archive/13.08/2001_pr.html

The iPod Evangelist: Steve Jobs (2002)
www.wired.com/wired/archive/13.08/2002_pr.html

The Candidate: Howard Dean (2003)
www.wired.com/wired/archive/13.08/2003_pr.html

The Celebrity Blogger: Ana Marie Cox (2004-05)
www.wired.com/wired/archive/13.08/2004_pr.html

The Birth of Google
www.wired.com/wired/archive/13.08/battelle_pr.html

Reprinted from Assignment Zero:

Did Assignment Zero Fail? A Look Back, and Lessons Learned
www.wired.com/print/techbiz/media/news/2007/07/ assignment_zero_final

The Experts at the Periphery
www.wired.com/print/techbiz/media/news/2007/07/ academics_crowdsourcing

News the Crowd Can Use
www.wired.com/print/techbiz/media/news/2007/07/ news_users_use

Exploring the Dark Side of Crowdsourcing
www.wired.com/print/techbiz/media/news/2007/07/ tricksters

Forty Strangers in a Virtual Room Talk About Religion
www.wired.com/print/techbiz/media/news/2007/07/ open_source_religion

What Does Crowdsourcing Really Mean?
www.wired.com/print/techbiz/media/news/2007/07/ crowdsourcing

Using Crowd Power for R&D
www.wired.com/print/techbiz/media/news/2007/07/ crowdsourcing_diversity

Crowdsourcing Soccer in the U.K.
www.wired.com/print/techbiz/media/news/2007/07/ crowdsourcing_soccer

We're All Mac Users Now (by Leander Kahney, 2004)
www.wired.com/print/gadgets/mac/news/2004/01/61730

Books (available online)

Benkler, Yochai. *The Wealth of Networks: How Social Production Transforms Markets and Freedom.* New Haven, Conn.: Yale UP, 2006.

Von Hippel, Eric. *Democratizing Innovation.* Cambridge, Mass: MIT Press, 2005.

YRUHRN. (Crowdsourced book created by One Thousand People.) Lifebushido Publishing, 2006. Available online at *http://yruhrn.com/book/*

Books (full text not available online)

Anderson, Chris. *The Long Tail: Why the Future of Business is Selling Less of More.* New York: Hyperion, 2006.

Barringer and Ireland. *Entrepreneurship: Successfully Launching New Ventures* (2nd ed). Upper Saddle River, N.J.: Pearson Prentice Hall, 2007.

Christensen, Clayton M. *The Innovator's Dilemma.* New York: HarperCollins, 2003.

Christensen, Karen and David Levinson Eds. *Encyclopedia of Community: From the Village to the Virtual World.* Thousand Oaks, Calif. SAGE Publications, 2003.

Cornwall, Jeffrey R., DAvid O.Vang, David & Jean M. Hartman. *Entrepreneurial Financial Management: An Applied Approach.* Upper Saddle River, N.J.: Pearson Prentice Hall, 2004.

Farrell, Larry. *Getting Entrepreneurial!: Creating and Growing Your Business in the 21st Century.* Hoboken, N.J: John Wiley & Sons, Inc., 2003.

Foot, David K. with Daniel Stoffman. *Boom, Bust & Echo: How to Profit from the Coming Demographic Shift*. Toronto: Macfarlane Walter & Ross, 1996.

Friedman, Thomas L. *The World is Flat: The Globalized World in the Twenty-First Century*. London: Penguin Books, 2005.

Libert, B., and Jon Spector, and thousands of contributors. *We are Smarter Than Me: How to Unleash the Power of Crowds in your Business*. Upper Saddle River, N.J.: Pearson Education, 2008.

Mackay, Charles LL.D. *Extraordinary Popular Delusions & The Madness of Crowds*, Updated Edition With a Foreword by Andrew Tobias. New York: Three Rivers Press, 1980.

McCraw, Thomas K. *Prophet of Innovation: Joseph Schumpeter and Creative Destruction*. Cambridge, Mass.: Harvard University Press, 2007

Powazek, Derek M. *Design for Community: The Art of Connecting Real People in Virtual Places*. Berkeley: New Riders, 2001.

Putnam, Robert D. *Bowling Alone: The Collapse and Revival of American Community*. New York: Simon & Schuster, 2000.

Renninger, K. Ann, and Wesley Shumar Eds. *Building Virtual Communities: Learning and Change in Cyberspace (Learning in Doing: Social, Cognitive and Computational Perspectives)*. New York: Cambridge UP, 2002.

Rheingold, Howard. *Smart Mobs*. Cambridge, Mass.: Perseus Books, 2002.

———. *The Virtual Community*. New York: Harper Collins, 1994.

Rushkoff, Douglas. *Get Back in the Box: How Being Great at What You Do Is Great for Business*. New York: HarperCollins, 2005.

Sawyer, Keith. *Group Genius: The Creative Power of Collaboration*. Cambridge, Mass.: Perseus, 2007.

Schumpeter, Joseph. *Capitalism, Socialism and Democracy* (3rd ed), New York: Harper and Brothers. 1950.

Silver, David. *Smart Start-Ups: How Entrepreneurs and Corporations Can Profit by Starting Online Communities.* Hoboken, N.J.: John Wiley and Sons, 2007.

Surowiecki, James. *The Wisdom of Crowds.* New York: Doubleday, 2004. Excerpt at *www.randomhouse.com/features wisdomofcrowds/ excerpt.htm.* Q&A with author also available at *wisdomofcrowds/ Q&A.htm.*

Taylor, William C. and Polly LaBarre. *Mavericks at Work: Why the Most Original Minds in Business Win.* New York: HarperCollins, 2006.

Timmons, Jeffrey and Stephen Spinelli. *New Venture Creation: Entrepreneurship for the 21st Century* (7th ed). New York: McGraw-Hill, 2007.

Weber, Larry. *Marketing to the Social Web: How Digital Customer Communities Build Your Business.* Hoboken, N.J.: John Wiley & Sons, 2007.

Magazine Articles

Allison, Kevin. "Cisco's chief places his next online bet." *Financial Times* (July 16, 2007) 13.

Beaumont, Claudine. "TechCrunch shows off the best of renewed 'Web 2.0.'" *Vancouver Sun* (September 28, 2007) C4.

Bradbury, Danny. "12 Months —8 Predictions." *Backbone* (January/ February 2008) 32–9.

Bricklin, Dan. "The Cornucopia of the Commons: How to get volunteer labor." *www.bricklin.com/cornucopia.html.* Viewed October 1, 2007.

Catone, Josh. "Crowdsourcing: A Million Heads Is Better Than One." March 22, 2007. Read/WriteWeb. *www.readwriteweb.com/ archives/crowdsourcing_million_heads.* Viewed July 1, 2007.

Grossman, Lev. "Time's Person of the Year: You." *Time* December 13, 2006. *http://www.time.com/time/magazine/article/0,9171,1569514,00.html*. Viewed March, 2008.

Hedlund, Mark. "Making the web into a banking platform (whether they like it or not)". O'Reilly Radar. July 25, 2007.

Howe, Jeff. "The Rise of Crowdsourcing." *Wired Magazine* (June 14, 2006). *www.wired.com/wired/archive/14.06/crowds.html*. Viewed March, 2008.

Lam, Kempton, and Nisan Gabbay. "iStockphoto Case Study: Howe to evolve from a free community site to a successful business." November 26, 2006. *http://startup-review.com/blog/istockphoto-case-study-how-to-evolve-from-a-free-community-to-a-successful-business.php*. Viewed October 1, 2007.

Lee-Young, Joanne. "News site secures landmark funding." *Vancouver Sun* (July 30, 2007), E31.

McCarthy, Caroline. "Microsoft acquire equity stake in Facebook, expands ad partnership." CNet News. *www.news.com/8301-13577_3-9803872-36.html*. Viewed March, 2008

McGirt, Ellen. "Hacker. Dropout. CEO." *Fast Company* (May 2007, Issue 115, p. 74). *www.fastcompany.com/magazine/115/open_features-hacker-dropout-ceo.html*. Viewed, March 2008.

"NowPublic.com Closes $10.6 Million Series A Financing Led by Rho Ventures and Rho Canada." July 30, 2007. *http://mtippett.wordpress.com/2007/07/30/nowpubliccom-closes-106-million-series-a-financing-let-by-rho-ventures-and-rho-canada*. Viewed August 10, 2007.

———. "What is Web 2.0: Design Patterns and Business Models for the Next Generation of Software." O'Reilly (September 30, 2005) *http://www.oreilly.com/pub/a/oreilly/tim/news/2005/09/30/what-is-web-20.html*.

O'Reilly, Tim. "Emerson and Oliver Wendell Holmes." O'Reilly Radar *(September 2, 2007).* *http://radar.oreilly.com/archives/2007/09/emerson_and_oli_1.html.*

"Our Approach," Rho Ventures. *www.rho.com/venture_capital/about_vc/vc_approach.html.* Viewed March, 2008.

"S-Commerce: Beyond MySpace and YouTube." *Spark!* October 2006. www.competeinc.com/research/spark/Archive. Viewed January 13, 2008.

"Top Ten Crowdsourcing Companies." *Innovation Zen.* August 1, 2006. *www.innovationzen.com/blog/2006/08/01/top-10-crowdsourcing-companies.* Viewed July 1, 2007.

"2006 Fast 50—Bruce Livingstone, iStockphoto," from *http://fastcompany.com/fast50_06/profile/?livingstone314.* Viewed October 2, 2007.

"Top Ten Crowdsourcing Companies." From *http://innovationzen.com/blog/2006/08/01/top-10-crowdsourcing-companies.*

Index

About the Author

Richard J. Goossen, PhD, is the founder of Crowdpreneur Networks, Inc. (*www.crowdpreneur.com*) and CEO of M & A Capital Corporation (*www.MandACapital.com*). He is also an adjunct professor of entrepreneurship and the founder and director of the Centre for Entrepreneurial Leaders, Trinity Western University (Greater Vancouver, BC, Canada).

Rick has more than 20 years of experience as a strategy, finance, and growth consultant. He has been a director, officer, advisor, and shareholder of/for a number of companies in the following business sectors: financial services, pharmaceuticals, medical device technology, wireless internet, IT training and online education, online travel and loyalty programs, e-business systems integration, computer hardware distribution, application service providers, software development, resource and mining, property development, and management consulting.

Rick's education includes the following: a PhD from Middlesex University, London, UK; a masters degree of law (LLM) from Columbia University, New York City; a bachelor's degree of laws (LLB) (Hons) from McGill University, Montreal; and a bachelor's degree of arts (BA) (Hons) (First Class) from Simon Fraser University, Vancouver.

In addition, Rick is a professional public speaker. He has had countless speaking engagements in Europe, North America, and Asia. He has also written four books, including *The Christian Entrepreneur: Insights From the Marketplace*, and *The Practice of Entrepreneurail Thinking abd Learning*, edited three books, and written more than 120 articles for diverse publications throughout the world, from leading academic journals to trade magazines and newspapers. A few of the most pertinent articles are "Bringing 'the Entrepreneurial Practices Ways' to the Big Companies: An Interview with Larry Farrell," "The Entrepreneur, From Classroom to the Field: An Interview with Murray Low," and "Entrepreneurship: Education and Success," all featured in the *Journal of Business Strategy*. His most recent books include *Entrepreneurial Excellence: Profit from the Best Ideas of the Experts* (The Career Press, 2007), and *Entrepreneurial Leaders: Reflections on Faith at Work*, Vol. 3(TWU Press, 2007).